POTS
FOR ALL SEASONS

POTS

FOR ALL SEASONS

Tom Harris

PIMPERNEL
PRESS LTD
www.pimpernelpress.com

PAGE 2 A bold display of hellebores and heucheras is set off among other pots containing thyme, scillas, houseleeks and skimmia in a balance of textures, shapes and shades.

RIGHT The right plant in the perfect pot achieves a whole that adds up to much more than the sum of its parts. Here coreopsis and uncinia team up in a particularly complementary container.

Contents

THE JOYS OF GROWING PLANTS IN POTS

An introduction to pots

The first plant I ever confined to a pot was a brilliant scarlet-flowered *Rhododendron* 'Britannia'. Kaleidoscopic drifts of rhododendrons, encountered during a family holiday, left an indelible impression on my eight-year-old self and I was so unstoppably determined to grow one back home that the unsuitable alkaline soil of my parents' garden seemed a minor obstacle. Happily, my nan's all-knowing gardening encyclopaedia obliged with a tenable solution: plant in tubs of ericaceous (acidic or lime-free) compost and water often (using rainwater). And so occurred my first brush with the practice of container gardening.

In my earliest growing years, I firmly believed that planting direct into the earth was the only sensible way. I thought stuffing plants in pots unkind and impure. That must-have rhododendron was a very rare exception.

I had been sold on gardening from the first moment I wielded a trowel. As children, we are fascinated by the tiniest workings of nature; then, sadly, most of us lose interest during the approach to adulthood. Others like me, however, grow ever more enthralled. Even at a young age, I understood that gardening – and all that it entailed – was productive and fulfilling. When tending the tiny but excitingly promise-filled rectangle of garden entrusted to me by my mum, I became immersed in a world of living marvel. I engaged totally with the plants, soil and wondrous creatures that, whether aiding or hindering my efforts, roamed this precious Lilliputian domain. It was my personal slice of the planet and I loved it. Visits to open gardens and flower shows – the floral marquees always mind-bogglingly diverse in content – fuelled my desire to explore the nurturing world of horticulture. Equal to my enchantment with nature and the thrill of growing was an intense attraction to all things colourful. Unsurprising, then, that the encounters with those vibrant rhododendrons and awe-inspiring banks of perfect flower-show blooms had such profound influence.

It wasn't until I was confronted with a rocky, almost soilless garden in my teens that pots again leapt heroically to my aid. Gardening on shallow, stony soil overlying rock is a test for any cultivator of plants and planting with a pickaxe is not an approach to perpetuate. Shifting a few planters around seemed far less backbreaking than hours spent chipping away at rock to achieve inadequately sized planting pockets. In this hard place, growing in pots was the blindingly obvious fix.

PREVIOUS PAGE Pots allow you to position plants requiring very different soil conditions side by side, achieving exciting pictures not possible in the ground. Here dry-loving echeverias sit below a potted corkscrew willow.

LEFT Soilless spaces can be speedily and dramatically transformed using plants in pots. Container gardening can become an obsession!

PLACES FOR POTS

The welcoming world of container gardening, with its limitless potential and numerous virtues, opened its doors to me. I entered and became engrossed, obsessed, even possessed. At the advanced age of fifteen, I realized that planting in pots was a pursuit that engaged me mentally, physically, emotionally and creatively. It still does: I'm ever discovering new plants and the possible combinations are unending; the activity keeps me fit; and there are many moments of elation, healthily balanced by occasional disappointment and drama. Most significantly, though, this style of growing has become my primary creative outlet and therapy of choice.

This strand of gardening is not just for the retired or those with time on their hands or, of course, only for garden owners. Not least because it can be so readily and successfully pursued in even the tiniest and most inhospitable spaces – from windowsills and walls to up on a roof or down in a dingy basement courtyard – container growing stands accessibly apart from other forms of gardening. As decades of first-hand experience have taught me, growing plants in pots extends many opportunities,

Containers allow us to present and enjoy our favourite plants in lively and intimate ways, elevating them in the best light and to maximum advantage.

both in terms of creativity and cultivation, not on offer to those growing exclusively in the ground.

Containers allow us to present and enjoy our favourite plants in lively and intimate ways, elevating them in the best light and to maximum advantage. There's thrill when the right plant or plants are married to the perfect pot in the most complementary setting. At its most potent, this synergetic relationship delivers a whole that far exceeds the sum of parts. In my view, container gardening is a particularly inclusive form of artistic expression, in which almost anyone can not only participate but succeed, deriving enormous pleasure and satisfaction from both the process and the end result. Achieve a modicum of success and there's a fair chance you'll be hooked. I've seen many previously unconvinced friends become so.

Potted gardens are scalable in all respects, including the time and effort required, and so even within the constraints of a busy modern lifestyle they offer a viable way of greening up your surroundings. Tending your own bit of green space, if only for ten minutes here and there, is an increasingly recognized antidote to excessive screen gazing, tiring commutes and artificial environments.

You can become a container gardener at any point in life. You can go out tomorrow and buy a pot or two (or find objects to repurpose), some fresh compost and a few good-looking plants. They needn't cost a fortune. Half an hour or so of calming compost fondling and creative arranging later and, in addition to the enjoyment of the doing, you'll have gained a display that, with a little therapeutic tending, will bring weeks or months of pleasure.

Perhaps most advantageously, containers offer the chance to create displays with considerable flexibility and freedom. Most pots are easily portable and so can be moved, rearranged or regrouped whenever the need or whim arises. That impulsive desire to shake things up and change the view grabs me often and a couple of hours spent reshuffling a group of pots is the most restorative tonic I know. It's instantly gratifying and genuinely spirit lifting.

There are other advantages too. It is preferable to wait until a plant unhappily positioned in the ground is dormant before moving it. Growing it in a container, you can shift the same plant without disruption whenever, wherever and as often as you like. Thanks to this relative portability, plants in pots can go with you when moving home. Plants growing in the garden are mostly regarded as fixtures, whereas those in pots are usually considered possessions. This is especially

LEFT Containers are a sensible option for those who don't own the plot they tend: plants in pots can go with you when you move, and allow you to get straight back to growing. Hostas, dwarf hebes, thymes and lavenders are all easily transportable.

BELOW In pots the very best of every season can be brought close by. In early spring dwarf irises and narcissi oblige.

relevant to a generation for whom it is proving difficult to climb on the property ladder and for others who rent but, understandably, prefer not to invest heavily in beautifying a garden they don't own. So attached to their gorgeous collection of planted pots were they that friends of mine took full advantage of this transportability when they moved from England to France and then, after a couple of years, back again. Certainly not a cheap exercise, but compared to the time, effort and financial outlay of replacing them, very cost effective. Most beneficially, though, their bare French courtyard was speedily and familiarly beautified. On whatever scale, there are many positives in having the choice to take your garden when you up sticks. Some plants are expensive, while others, like many of my own, have sentimental attachment.

BELOW LEFT Potted into terracotta, insectivorous plants, including handsome sarracenias, can be provided the damp conditions in which they thrive and given more shelter in winter.

BELOW Displays composed of planted pots are easy to expand or contract, depending on season and your own schedule. In spring, the more tulips the merrier!

I was halfway through taking the photographs for this book when disaster struck and unforeseen building work forced me to shift every last pot – mid-growing season – to another location. It was no mean feat, but within just a few days, my planted containers made a barren and uninviting concreted and gravelled yard appear as if it had forever been a garden. The buzz of the creative challenge more than cancelled out the stress and this pop-up oasis soothed away the inevitable aches. If the evacuated space had been a 'dig up' garden or an inadvertently flattened one, the plants and I would still be recovering from the trauma. Proof, if proof were needed, that if you grow plants in pots, you can create a life-enhancing, flower-filled, leafy haven anywhere.

REASONS TO GROW IN POTS

- **Convenience** Even the tiniest and most uninviting spaces can be speedily transformed – without huge investment – using planted containers. Plants in season can be brought comfortably near.

- **Creativity** Container gardening is an artistic pursuit that anyone can try and triumph with. Experimenting with plant and pot combinations is pleasurable and the results highly rewarding.

- **Design** Containers can be dramatic focal points, repeated elements in a scheme or used to create a particular feel. In places where there is no soil, they are a godsend.

- **Flexibility** You can expand or slim down a container display depending on the season or your time. Plantings past their prime are easily swapped with those at peak.

- **Therapy** Tending in the fresh air, for however short a time, is a proven stress buster. Pots allow especially intimate contact with and a greater appreciation of plants.

- **Transportability** Plants in containers are easily moved from one area of the garden to another and can be taken with you when you move home.

- **Variety** Pots allow you to grow a wider range of plants, including those unsuited to your garden soil or which need cold-weather protection.

A CREATIVE THERAPY

However difficult the space, there are appealing plants – and attractive pots – to adorn it. Appointed thoughtfully and cared for appropriately, planted containers are an invaluable addition to any plot and essential to some. Plants in pots can enliven areas within a garden, such as paved patios, shady corners and dry patches at the base of a hedge, that are otherwise difficult to colonize. They can equally camouflage or obscure an eyesore, screen off a play area, flexibly delineate or assist in creating a fresh vista. They can provide an eye-drawing finishing touch, be a key element in the overall design or serve as a starting point around which even an entire garden can be developed. In some instances they can be emotionally provocative. Humour should definitely be on the garden agenda. Many pots, including elegant olive jars and classical urns, beauteous objects in their own right, can be handsome, unplanted focal points. Whether your taste is for regimented formality, minimalism or, as in my case, quirky eclecticism, all are attainable, courtesy of

However difficult the space, there are appealing plants – and attractive pots – to adorn it.

carefully selected plants and containers. In fact, you can accomplish a certain 'look', mood or theme in just a single pot. Oh, the possibilities!

I've endured some uncomfortable periods without a garden. These were mercifully short but even the briefest time deprived of personal growing space serves to confirm that tending plants and engaging with green can significantly improve our well-being. At these times, my pots were distributed among the gardens of various friends to be later reassembled and rapidly transform each new-to-me garden.

I wish I could claim that memorable red rhododendron is still going strong, but it isn't. Nor, thankfully, does its unflattering plastic pot still exist. The gardening industry has developed in leaps and bounds during the half century since my prized shrub was young. The range of plants offered for container culture and the variety of receptacles to grow them

ABOVE LEFT Pots offer opportunity to experiment with textures and shapes within any size of space.

LEFT In pots, diminutive beauties such as gentians can be met nearer eye level in order to admire their intricacies.

RIGHT Singling out architectural plants, such as phormiums, and siting them where the sun strikes them side on results in brilliant lighting effects.

in have expanded and improved enormously. It has never been a finer time to be a grower of plants in pots.

That long-gone rhododendron secured me an early understanding of the differing needs of plants and highlighted that, in containers, you can readily customize and regulate their growing conditions. Naturally, this temptingly enables you to try many plants that are otherwise unsuited to your garden, including those that are opposed to your soil type. My red rhodo is the perfect example. In pots you can grow plants that thrive in damp conditions, even though your soil is sandy and fast draining, or vice versa; and, of course, all the many variations on that theme. Living in pots, less winter-hardy plants, from bananas to tree ferns, can augment the display all summer, then be moved with relative ease to a more protected location during cold weather. For some this might be too much effort, but among the merits of container gardening is that you can keep it as simple or make it as complex and involved as suits you. There are inevitably a few limitations and demands (the higher level of aftercare than in a border, for instance) but these are far outweighed by the creative and life-enriching rewards.

PUSHING BOUNDARIES

Containers allow us to grow plants that require contrasting soil conditions harmoniously side by side in separate pots, so the scope for stunning plant associations is greatly broadened. By appreciating their specific needs and caring for them accordingly, moisture-loving hostas may flourish in proximity to drought-tolerant lavenders, and ericaceous pieris can neighbour lime-preferring clematis. Desert succulents will thrive cheek-to-cheek with moisture-reliant insectivorous plants, while prairie grasses sit happily alongside bog sedges. Such plant get-togethers are not generally possible in the garden proper. But don't dismiss this as cheating, as I once did. A resolutely purist attitude can limit creativity. Rather, it is licensed manipulation and advantage taking. When growing plants in confinement, we are often compelled to push the boundaries and experiment. It's a stimulating element of the art, craft and practice of container gardening.

Besides, there are many plants that I'm happy to grow in pots but there's no chance I'd let them loose. *Phalaris arundinacea* a vigorously spreading variegated grass is a classic, – it simply won't stay still; mints likewise. Fast-spreading bamboos and other plants that are too rampant and ill-behaved to be offered free rein in the garden can be enjoyed for all their virtues without concern for their bad habits.

In pots, plants deserving of close attention, including those that are aromatic or invitingly tactile, can be sited close to seats, paths, doors and other locations for effortless and regular appreciation (and, of course, replaced when past their prime). Equally, diminutive plants, such as alpines, may be brought conveniently near to eye level in order to admire their fine detail. To be greeted by terracotta pots full of scented lilies each time you step outside your front door is life enriching. So is opening a window to inhale the heady perfume of sweet peas brought near in

RIGHT Raised up on a variety of impromptu plinths, maples, tulips, hostas, saxifrages, primulas and other spring reliables are displayed together in a thrilling jumble. A joy you can only achieve so readily and flexibly using plants growing in pots.

Gardening with pots is about developing pleasing, nourishing spaces and unlocking your own creative potential.

a large glazed container. Because it obligingly allows us to have our cherished plants more appreciably close for more of the time, gardening in containers could easily be hailed as the most intimate growing option. Bees buzzing in a border are one thing but frequenting salvias in a pot on your doorstep is altogether more personal.

Whatever their scale, gardens housed in containers are absorbing, life improving and accessible. Growing in pots is an ongoing experiment full of reward that delivers on so many levels. It's about developing pleasing, nourishing spaces and unlocking your own creative potential. It's not essential to become enslaved to your containers. I may container-grow to excess, but you can take away from this book as little or as much as suits you. There's no mystery, no baffling science and little in the way of barriers. All you need to get started and succeed is a basic understanding of what enables a plant to thrive, a bit of time, a spark of inspiration and plenty of willingness. The following pages are a lively concoction of plant and pot suggestions, gentle guidance and considered, experience-based opinion. Bring to bear your own personal expression and taste.

Fundamentally, if your potted garden brings you pleasure, that is all that really matters.

MAKING PICTURES

The practice of cultivating plants involves both science and technique, but the creation of a garden is a personal artistic outlet. I've long considered ornamental gardening to be a form of picture making. A garden of containers is perhaps more still life – or collage – than landscape but the same aesthetic principles can be applied to both picture art and garden making. The creator plays with colour, shape, texture, scale and proportion to compose a captivating, emotionally provocative view.

Gardens are additionally rendered in (at least) three dimensions, are multi-sensory, always evolving and ever changing through the seasons. Obligingly, container gardens are also supremely flexible in both configuration and scale. This is art where any gardener, 'artistic' or not, can flex full creative control. You can create a themed display, applying a host of rules and principles, or bypass that, follow your eye and make it up as you go. Best results come usually from treading a line between these two approaches: have an understanding of how or why a particular arrangement is successful but always retain the freedom to explore and experiment. Experimentation is more than half the pleasure and very often getting it a little wrong is key to getting it spot on next time.

With picture making in mind, this chapter explores, in brief, the creative considerations of container gardening, from using colour to displaying your plants to greatest effect.

LEFT Varying materials, heights and textures but a limited palette create a scene that moves your eye gently from one point of interest to the next without being too overwhelming. The repetition and distribution of certain plants, including echeverias, purple-mauve nemesias and yellow-leaved sedum, binds the picture.

RIGHT Raising pots and decorative items up to eye level provides a different viewpoint and allows for closer inspection of smaller intricate plants.

Moods and themes

Haphazard groups of planted pots can be perfectly presentable, but a co-ordinated approach more reliably achieves a pleasing result. Many of my own groups have gathered piecemeal over time but every now and again I spend a therapeutic hour or two making better sense of them.

Through thoughtful teaming of pots, plants and accessories, it is easy to summon an evocative atmosphere. Even a stand-alone pot, perhaps lime washed and filled with bougainvillea, evoking the Mediterranean, can conjure a distinct feel but clusters of pots offer the greatest thematic scope. They may stir treasured memories, reflect a particular gardening style such as 'cottage' or 'prairie', or adhere to a colour scheme. They may celebrate a season or a single genus or type of plant, such as pelargoniums or succulents. The simpler and subtler themes are usually more comfortable to live with, though: it's easy to tire of overstated ones. There is no need to conform slavishly to a particular theme. Much enjoyment derives from personal interpretation and blending your own notions with inspiration from books, magazines, gardens, holidays, flower shows or social media. Even a stroll along the beach or in the countryside can provide a wealth of ideas – and props – for your container garden.

BELOW Groups of containers can create a particular atmosphere, be obviously themed or simply celebrate a season. This gathering shouts of late spring.

By thoughtful addition, subtraction or substitution of components, you can change the emphasis or entire feel of a scene composed of potted plants, with only a restricted palette of materials. A group of bold-leaved hostas and whiskery grasses held in weathered terracotta will form a textural tapestry of leafy contrast: the rigid, rugged-leaved hostas tempered by the wispy, flowing grasses. If the site is slightly shady, a few ferns will increase texture, while in full sun one or two succulents will ramp up the sculptural element. Contribute a Japanese maple (acer), a dwarf bamboo and a few small boulders to the shady scene and an oriental air descends. A handful of pebbles, lengths of gnarled driftwood and perhaps a young dwarf fan palm (*Chamaerops humilis*), mulched with seashells, will give the sunny version a maritime slant. Remove the hostas, replacing them with softer, daisy-flowered tender perennials, such as argyranthemums, and that scene becomes more relaxed and airy. Restricting yourself to just one or two varieties each of the hostas and grasses, then repeating them in a row of symmetrically arranged, square, grey terrazzo or metal holders, instead of terracotta, will achieve a more formal, contemporary result. And so it goes on: the possibilities for adaption and reinvention of your container scenes are unending.

ABOVE LEFT Pots offer a flexible way of displaying collections of certain types of plant such as succulents. Individually potted, they can be moved around to incorporate new additions.

LEFT Bold, spiky plants including cordylines and phormiums are emphasized when set among Japanese maples and other plants with soft, feathery leaves. Despite the dramatic contrast, the use of predominantly foliage plants achieves a calm look.

The Setting

Backgrounds play a vital role in showing off plants in pots: they have the power to enhance or diminish. Their setting should emphasize containers, not overwhelm them. Relating pots comfortably to their surroundings, by echoing the colours, shapes and textures of building materials, paving and general planting, will ensure they reach their full visual potential.

Most often, containers form a link between the home and the main body of a garden, although sometimes they *are* the garden. They may form a cheery welcoming party at the door or adorn paved areas, terraces and decks. Large sculptural containers can serve as stand-alone focal points, injecting an otherwise bland space with colour and drama. In designer gardens, they are often a fundamental of the plan, contributing rhythm and structure, but normally pots are brought in to beautify an existing space and make it more intimate and inviting.

Containers are generally used in close context only with their immediate surroundings. It is possible to create a scene, secreted on the other side of a hedge, fence or wall, that is different in style to the rest of the garden, thus providing a change of pace and emphasis. Within a tranquil leafy oasis, a screened-off area bursting with unexpected riotous colour, courtesy of canna, coleus and petunia-filled containers, will have great impact. Equally, in a garden that overflows with colour, a tucked-away corner furnished with pots of calm leafiness and muted tints offers respite. Such contrasts need not always be hidden. A pop of unashamedly bright colour can impose triumphantly, in plain sight, on an otherwise gentle, green oasis; containers offer an easy way of achieving this and opportunity to experiment.

Containers can fill temporary gaps in beds and borders or rest there more permanently. You can either disguise the pot itself among the border plants or make a full-blown feature by choosing an attractive pot that both enhances and is set off by the surrounding planting. A bold-leaved variegated yucca or agave housed in a rugged terracotta or stone pot, for instance, will form a strong textural and visual contrast when sitting among an airy planting of *Erigeron karvinskianus*.

Not every garden boasts attractive existing backdrops, such as stone or brick walls, and sometimes a bespoke 'set' is called for. These don't necessarily have to be elaborate and may be as simple as a few reclaimed floorboards fixed to the garage wall or an interestingly weathered sheet of corrugated iron. Feature trellis or a well-finished fencing panel can be erected, with thought not just for privacy or shelter but also to form a fitting foil to your plants in containers. Likewise, a rendered block wall can be a useful and attractive feature and will present an exciting blank canvas. To build a wall just to show off a collection of pots may seem an

KEEP IT SIMPLE

Busy pots filled with flowers will stand out better against unfussy backdrops. Variegated leaves also require a simple foil: variegated set against variegated presents a messy picture. A plain wall or fence, however, will calmly emphasize them. It stands to reason that light-coloured blooms require a darker background to make them stand out and vice versa.

extreme measure but, if cleverly integrated, it can be a major feature, creating a new environment in which you can grow plants you previously could not. Rendered walls can be painted any shade and repainted every now and then to set off different themes or plants. A wall painted in dusky terracotta is suggestive of the Mediterranean, whereas bright blue is Moroccan in flavour and blue-green will summon up a seaside feel. Sheds are often less-than-attractive features, yet, gently customized, they can make worthy canvases for collections of pots and arty pieces that in turn can convincingly relate them to the rest of the garden. Indeed, I've always relished the creative potential of garden sheds.

Horizontal surfaces also play their part. The base on which containers sit will, like the backdrop, contribute to the overall appearance. Paving, gravel and timber decking are most often used for garden flooring and the existing surface will, in conjunction with the background, influence your choice of container. A crisp, modern-looking hard area, composed of reconstituted granite-effect paving, most reliably works with contemporary metal, repeated, square terrazzo planters and architectural planting. A courtyard paved with random-sized warm Indian sandstone more often suits informally brimming terracotta or timber. Grey or white terrazzo is considerably enhanced when standing on a carpet of blue-grey slate chips, especially if they are repeated as a mulch atop the compost. Lead-effect fibreglass troughs look most appealing against the warmth of red-brick paviours.

ABOVE LEFT This froth of *Erigeron karvinskianus* and pink argyranthemum spilling from a strongly patterned pot is set against a plain backdrop in order to reach its full visual potential.

LEFT A simple neutral background of vertical wooden planks may be all that is necessary to help your containers and the plants in them stand out.

RIGHT When set with planted pots, rusting garden implements come to life. Parsley, rocket, pelargoniums and peppers are shown off here among bold pieces of aged iron.

Colour

Opportunity to play with colour is a thrilling prospect. We are all profoundly, albeit often subconsciously, influenced by colour. In our gardens, colour is often the dominant visual element and the most considered. It can play spatial tricks, and affect both mood and perception: a space may feel larger or smaller, calm or exciting, warm or cool, and objects may appear nearer or more distant, depending on colour. The notion that I could grow flowers in any colour first lured me to gardening and that thrill is kept alive by constant new plant introductions offering blooms – and leaves – in an ever-widening palette.

An uncoordinated sweet-shop mix of colours can be victorious, but serious clashes may hamper the overall view. Restraining your palette is often a greater guarantee of visual success, particularly in confined spaces. The more colours you add, the more diluted will be the final effect. One tip is even distribution: repetition of the same colours (or shades of them) through a planting gains a more unified, soothing feel.

Favourite colours are a sound basis for any scheme and especially monochromatic themes. Limiting to variants of a single colour ensures a harmonious whole; bringing together dark and light hues of the same colour achieves a sense of depth. Each individual colour also has its own particular subliminal consequence (mauve, for example, is quieting, while red is more stimulating). Colour schemes may be muted and soothing or exuberant and energizing, and to varying degrees. Colours that are in harmony have a positive effect. Jarring colours stop us in our tracks.

Visually, warm bright colours, including yellow and orange, advance toward us. They snap with vitality so are ideal for a party space or barbecue area. Soft pastels give the illusion of distance and pale hues are calming; they also reflect light and so are helpful in shade. By using foliage as a buffer, you can switch colour scheme from one pot to another, thus taking you from calm to lively and back again. Don't rely just on green leaves: bronze, silver or blue-grey can help the transition from hot to cool, light to dark and bright to pastel. Green is the most pacifying colour and not only does it offer an all-purpose backdrop in the form of hedges, trees and shrubs, but green flowers can unite colours otherwise at odds. Lime-green tobacco plants, for example, can marry intense shades of orange and pink for a really zingy display.

Containers also play a colour role, as do their surroundings. The warm, earthy tones of terracotta suit almost any planting scheme and setting. Silver metallic and grey terrazzo, however, are often more convincingly partnered by cooler pinks, blues, mauves, greys and white than by vibrant reds and yellows. Modern glazed containers are available in a variety of finishes and can contrast with or match their contents.

Be playful and experimental: colour is in the eye of the beholder.

UNDERSTANDING COLOUR

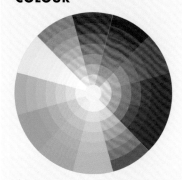

A colour wheel provides a basic demonstration of how the colours of the spectrum relate to and influence each other. Because they contain elements of their neighbours, adjacent colours blend and are referred to as 'harmonious'. 'Contrasting' colours appear on opposite sides of the wheel while those positioned at direct opposites, such as yellow and violet or red and green, create the most intense contrast and are referred to as 'complementary'. The wheel can also be split in two with cool colours (blues, greens and blue-purples) on one side and warmer colours (reds, oranges and yellows) on the other.

FAR LEFT Colours that neighbour each other on the colour wheel associate harmoniously. Here purple alliums rise through a drift of pink polygonums.

LEFT Limiting your colour palette can have striking effect as with these creamy-white hellebores set against bronze phormium. The glazed pot also tones in.

BELOW Containers allow you to be more adventurous with colour than you might in the border. Tulipa 'Formosa' and *Camassia cusickii* are an electric spring pairing.

Composition

Growing in pots is a contrived method of cultivating plants but as such it offers unlimited creative potential. Containers enable us to display and enjoy our plants quite differently to those planted in a border, and how they are arranged is especially important to the overall visual effect. A successful composition involves plants, flowers, leaves, pots and accessories that interrelate pleasingly in terms of shape, scale and proportion, as well as colour and texture, so that each is shown off to best advantage within a balanced picture.

Besides obliging as singular focal points, pots can be symmetrically paired or mirrored (such as either side of a door); repeated (perhaps along a path); huddled together in tight clusters; or arranged in more well-spaced groups, where each is celebrated yet retains a close context with its companions. The last is how I display the majority of my own containers.

BELOW LEFT Spacing pots so that each is individually discernible yet has clear context in a group results in a lively visual and textural feast.

BELOW Repetition of shapes, textures and colours binds together a collection of containers and accessories. Here it's blue and green with the knots in the timber echoing the swirly concrete (yes, concrete!) ammonite.

RIGHT Employing a row of matching pots each containing the same plant (here *Hylotelephium cauticola* 'Coca-cola') is a simple eye-drawing tactic.

BALANCED PLANTINGS

There are various trusted blueprints for arranging plants within an individual pot. The simplest uses a single variety, but you can employ any number and any combination of plants with complementary habits: the aim usually being to strike a balance of horizontals and verticals. The more different plants you use, though, the more diluted is the overall effect and the more difficult it is to manage. I often adhere to the 'rule of three': an upright plant, a trailer or ground coverer and a filler that links the other two visually. The permutations, however, are endless.

I greatly appreciate the qualities of the pots themselves (all are carefully chosen) and relish the interplay between the plants, the pots and the setting. A little breathing space helps achieve inviting, layered displays, allows plants to develop and permits easier manoeuvring when rejigging collections of containers.

Unless formal in appearance, a well-composed scene typically includes containers of varying heights and sizes but not always differing shapes. Sticking predominantly to either angular or round pots more readily leads to a coherent finish, as does limiting the number of materials. An emphatic differentiation in size, though, makes for a more dynamic scene and the surface of large pots can offer a foil to plants growing in smaller containers in front. While taller plants are usually best towards the back or, if to be seen from all angles, the centre, it doesn't necessarily follow that the tallest container should be sited likewise. Indeed, proportionately tall pots can be used to lift lower-growing plants, while large specimens generally appear more stable in pots that are as wide as they are tall. Matching plant and pot so they appear in proportion is important.

The most reliable approach to realizing a stunning display is to select a few key pots – perhaps all the same style but in different sizes – among which others (and accessories) can be artfully placed. The main containers will help anchor the arrangement and may house permanent plants, while the supplementary pots can host more temporary, seasonally replaced contents. Using a single variety per pot and repeating the same plant (or similar-looking ones), or colour, have a unifying influence. Juxtaposing components assures a lively picture, so use huge pots with tiny, set rough textures against smooth and put bold solid forms to contrast with the softer. Step back occasionally to assess the composition from different angles and shunt the pots around until you are satisfied with the overall look. You can reconfigure them at any time.

Texture and tactility

In pots, the plants we adore are especially accessible to all our senses. Vegetables, fruits and edible flowers are convenient for picking or tasting, while scented blooms waft directly beneath our nostrils. Brought near, rustling grasses and rattling seed pods are more audible. Visually, not only do colour, form and scale excite, but so too the infinitely varied consistencies of leaves, flowers, stems, garden surfaces and, of course, the pots themselves. Sophisticated displays rely as much on texture and shape as colour, and textures lend depth and feeling to our gardens, tempting us to interact by appealing to our sense of touch.

Many plants plead to be smoothed and caressed, and who isn't curious to discover if a leaf is as papery, as leathery, as hairy or as smooth as it appears? A 'touchy-feely' relationship with your plants will assist you in fully appreciating all their qualities and, up close and personal, some deliver extra rewards. It is only when you rub or gently crush their leaves that the aroma of many herbs, such as thyme and lemon verbena, is most potent. Such are the de-stressing and therapeutic benefits of plant 'petting' that I strategically position pots of pat-as-you-pass plants, including mossy saxifrages and clipped box. Running your fingers through the silky tufts of *Stipa tenuissima*, a hardy perennial grass, is a sensual, calming experience. Then there's the springy corkscrew willow with flexible stems that I like to wobble when I'm near, and not only are the soft flower spikes of tiarellas (foam flower) irresistibly pattable, but brushing them lightly against your palm affirms the appropriateness of their common name.

From the soft, felted foliage and stems of *Verbascum bombyciferum* (mullein), through the coarsely ribbed, undulating leaves of hostas, to high-gloss evergreens such as bergenias and camellias, every plant displays a distinct texture and offers a tactile encounter. Do proceed with caution, though: some plant parts can irritate (or worse). Euphorbias (spurge) – for their milky sap – and brugmansias (angel's trumpet), as well as some primulas, come immediately to mind.

The upper and undersides of a leaf can be markedly different in look and feel. No better example is there than *Rhododendron yakushimanum*: this compact, rugged evergreen is a far more container-worthy choice than the ungainly large-flowered hybrids I grew as a child. Its handsome chunky leaves are tough like leather above, but lift one and you'll discover buff-coloured indumentum, a covering of fine hairs that are velvety in look and feel. Flowers too vary in texture. The overblown blooms of begonias are silky-petalled, while those of fleshy-leaved echeverias are distinctly waxy and seemingly artificial in both look and feel.

Grouping together plants with the same or similar textures, such as all smooth succulents or all furry-stemmed ferns, lends serenity,

TOP As they ascend to flower the cone-shaped rosettes of orostachys (Chinese dunce cap) are tempting to pat.

ABOVE Add other textures to a display with tactile objects such as recycled glass or smooth river-worn pebbles.

OPPOSITE, LEFT A garden is made up of greatly varying textures contributed not only by plants but also by surfaces and objects, both living and inanimate. A group of pots offers an easy way to experiment with textural contrasts.

ABOVE CENTRE Marry foreground and backdrop using shapes, colours and textures. The pebbles filling the gabion echo the stone wall, whilst the orange-red heuchera leaves and terracotta pick up the tones of the roof tiles.

ABOVE RIGHT Among the most attractive qualities of many ornamental grasses is their animated behaviour: they are seldom still. Some grasses I plant as much for their sway in a breeze as any other reason. In this respect, tactile *Stipa tenuissima* is eternally trusty.

whereas mixing them up creates a more eye-challenging and stimulating scene. Using extremes of leaf size and texture guarantees verdant drama: the bold, shiny, sculptural leaves of fatsia, for example, are greatly accentuated when set against the delicate, filigree foliage of cut-leaf Japanese maples.

The hard landscaping elements of a garden, including walls and floors, contribute a multitude of interesting surfaces to contrast with and complement leaf and bloom. A smooth wall or paving, for instance, will emphasize rough-faced containers or coarse-leaved plants and vice versa. Containers themselves introduce many textures and sensations from the sensual smoothness of polished marble or terrazzo to the less inviting graininess of concrete or unglazed earthenware. Weathering and ageing, too, bring textural stimulation: stone and terracotta become lichen-coated and metals oxidize. Lively weavings of varying textures beckon and engage us in many enticing ways.

Accessories

The impromptu acquisition of several dozen tiny lichen-clad clay pots and a handsome, but leaky, galvanized watering can long ago convinced me that the sparing use of props can yield delight. Decommissioned, the can rested decoratively amid a group of terracotta-housed grasses while, impractically dinky, the pots were variously stacked up and laid down unplanted. The visual contrasts of empty pots abutting planted, and earthy warm tones set against cool metallic, all nestled cosily among calm greenery, enchanted me.

Many characterful retired implements and quirky horticultural *objets* now wittily augment and complement my multifarious pot collection. None have I paid much for, although it is possible to spend large sums on authentic garden antiques and fine statuary. Rummaging for bargain 'gardenalia' is a rewarding activity in itself, as is salvaging and repurposing. Whether bought, scrounged or foraged, natural or manmade, incidental accessories can truly enhance. Agricultural salvage often suits cottage gardens, while mossy stones and log sections will sympathetically bolster potted ferns in a light-starved corner. Bold objects that have a strong, definite shape, such as vintage lawn rollers or pebbles and boulders, are most effectual. And be playful: even kitsch gnomes can have a place. Honestly.

Restraint is the operative word: a few carefully selected, strategically placed items will grab attention more successfully than a jumbled collection of unrelated bits and pieces. Too much clutter will detract from the containers rather than accentuate them, so don't feel you have to use everything you've gathered all at once in one space. My shed is filled with items waiting for their moment but very few of them will never make it into view.

LABEL THEM

Plant names – especially specific varieties – can easily slip the memory, if only temporarily, and so labelling really helps. Far from being ugly and distracting, many plant labels make an attractive addition, especially in pots. It's not difficult to make your own from a variety of materials, like slate, bamboo or copper tubing, and even when not in practical service they are worthy of display.

TOP Rescued from a skip and balancing a trio of terracotta-housed houseleeks, this rusty roller skate usually draws a smile.

MIDDLE Plant labels needn't be unattractive and, when not naming plants, can be stored in full view.

BOTTOM All manner of decorative items can be brought in to add character: from fossils and pebbles to driftwood and rope.

Raise them up

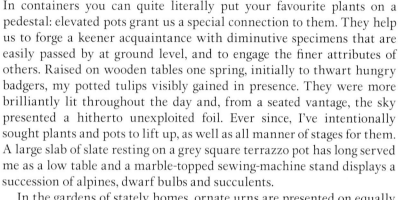

In containers you can quite literally put your favourite plants on a pedestal: elevated pots grant us a special connection to them. They help us to forge a keener acquaintance with diminutive specimens that are easily passed by at ground level, and to engage the finer attributes of others. Raised on wooden tables one spring, initially to thwart hungry badgers, my potted tulips visibly gained in presence. They were more brilliantly lit throughout the day and, from a seated vantage, the sky presented a hitherto unexploited foil. Ever since, I've intentionally sought plants and pots to lift up, as well as all manner of stages for them. A large slab of slate resting on a grey square terrazzo pot has long served me as a low table and a marble-topped sewing-machine stand displays a succession of alpines, dwarf bulbs and succulents.

In the gardens of stately homes, ornate urns are presented on equally impressive plinths and columns to aggrandize them. Most pots, though, require less monumental stands and, for reasons of weight and scale, small to medium-sized containers are more practically suited to being displayed off the ground. But don't raise just the tiniest pots: upraising larger ones among them will result in a more stimulating composition. Upturned galvanized dustbins (which also form capacious containers), old oil drums, garden chairs and wooden crates, among myriad others, are all fit for the purpose, whether for single pots or small gatherings. Upended sections of railway sleeper I've found ideal for showing off plants flowing from wall pots and wooden stepladders perfect for displaying rows of auriculas. Besides their practical purpose, such objects significantly enhance the picture, contributing textural contrasts and interesting shapes.

Not only can individual pots or small collections be admired on isolated podiums but gathered-together assortments on platforms of varied height and style achieve eclectic multi-level displays. Stacks of old house bricks are ideal for raising key pots within a group and also aiding drainage. A number of my own containers are dual purpose and are often used upside down to stand other pots atop. If you've room and ambition, stepped stacks of pallets faced up with decorative timber create 'islands' for larger congregations of containers.

ABOVE LEFT A slab of marble supported on brick pillars or an old sewing machine stand is an exemplary counter for a gaggle of pots and accompanying items.

BOTTOMLEFT When lifted well off the ground on the right plinth even just a small pot can have effect. Here *Isotoma* 'Fairy Footsteps' sits atop an upended, out-of-service drain grate.

SEASONAL
GALLERY

SPRING

SPRING BEGINS

An exciting time in the garden, spring is a swiftly unfolding season. Flowering bulbs are a mainstay and early on it's the shorter-growing species, predominantly blue and yellow ones, that are most abundant. These bulbs are well suited to growing in pots where they can be raised off the ground and admired in comfort. Nearly all my own dwarf bulbs find themselves in terracotta pots, pans or troughs, the warm tones of which show them off perfectly.

PAGE 32 It's possible to capture the essence of a season in a single well-planted pot, especially if you select plants synonymous with that time of year. *Gentiana sino-ornata* is one of the jewels of autumn and here is accompanied by October-flowering *Crocus speciosus* 'Conqueror'.

PREVIOUS PAGES The sudden power surge of late spring is evident in this potted landscape of at-their-peak tulips, flower-smothered cushions of phlox and ready-to-take-up-the-baton lavenders.

❶ Placed on an old dustbin and jam-packed, this container is on show from all angles. A single *Euphorbia* 'Redwing' in the centre will raise its vivid yellow-green flower bracts later. In the meantime, the plentiful flowers of *Primula* Gold-laced Group draw the eye. The heavy golden blooms of *Narcissus* 'Rip van Winkle' burst forth, tumble under their own weight and then nod in the slightest breeze.

❷ Following the same principle as the muscari (❹), this alternative features deep-blue *Scilla siberica* as partner to sempervivums. A hollow brick filled with gritty, free-draining compost offers just enough space to grow these diminutive plants.

❸ Dwarf irises flower during that transitional period when, all of a sudden, winter becomes spring. They are a 'must have'. When joined in bloom by miniature narcissi, you know spring has arrived. Here deep-blue *Iris reticulata* 'Harmony' and multi-headed *Narcissus* 'Tête-à-Tête' crowd around *Corylus avellana* 'Red Majestic', a spiral-stemmed contorted hazel, which throws striking shadows when set against the right background. Accompanying pots of porcelain-like *Iris* 'Katharine Hodgkin', violet. 'Pauline' and powder-blue 'Clairette' complete the scene.

❹ This simple but striking effect is achieved using *Muscari* 'Valerie Finnis' and a selection of hardy succulent sempervivums (houseleeks). Pot them in autumn and, come spring, the muscari will spear through the uneven sempervivum carpet, creating a visual treat of contrasting form and texture. Snip off dead muscari stems and, once they have withered, pull away the leaves to reveal a miniature rosette landscape.

❺ Packed into one of my favourite troughs, this is a cheery planting I repeat annually. *Anemone blanda* pushes up a succession of daisy-like blooms that complement the petal-weighted stars of *Narcissus* 'Rip van Winkle'. Bronze-leaved *Carex comans* lines up as a feathery backdrop.

HELLEBORES & HEUCHERAS

Both hellebores and heucheras are high on my list of reliable winter-into-spring container plants and they are superb partners. Heucheras work beautifully with a diverse range of plants so I use them frequently. They are often colourfully named: 'Silver Gilt' (dark-veined pewter-coloured leaves), 'Ginger Peach' (coppery-orange), 'Lime Ruffles', 'Plum Pudding' and 'Obsidian' are a few worth seeking. Sprays of dainty pink, cream or white flowers (depending on variety) appear intermittently through spring and summer.

My pick of hellebores for containers are Rodney Davey Marbled Group cultivars ❶ 'Dorothy's Dawn', ❷ 'Glenda's Gloss' and ❸ 'Moondance'. Their leaves are as handsome as their fine blooms and so, in common with heucheras, they offer year-round appeal. Also worth considering is apple-green-flowered *Helleborus foetidus*, a tough evergreen with elegant divided leaves. To get the best from them, feed potted hellebores every few weeks through late spring and summer, using a high-potash fertilizer. Where possible keep them in semi-shade, although they can be enjoyed in a more open position when in flower.

❹ Although past their dazzling peak, the bleaching saucer flowers of the hellebores remain subtly attractive and utterly magical when softly sunlit.

❺ For an early April colour boost, plant bulbs direct into the container in autumn or cheat a little and squeeze in a few tulips grown in 9cm (3½in) pots or from garden centres. Both hellebores and heucheras will cope with a little disturbance. 'Showcase', a short-growing, rich purple double tulip, sits well here.

❻ By mid-March, after two months of solid flowering, this trio of Rodney Davey Marbled Group hellebores are fading, but gracefully. Crowded into a vintage ammunition chest with an accompanying frill of purple-and-silver-leaved *Heuchera* 'Blackberry Jam' and raised on an old galvanized water tank, they are joined by the brick-housed sempervivums and scillas from page 36. The green winter buds of compact evergreen *Skimmia japonica* 'White Dwarf' open as starry, white spring flowers and the first of the tulips sidle into the background. Lichen-splattered terracotta, rusted metal, pebbles, clay tiles and weathered timber plinths offer a feast of interesting textures that would be diminished if there were too many flowers.

TULIPS WITH EVERYTHING

Mid- to late spring is tulip time. If you seek a punch of colour – and most of us do – plant tulips. Plant as many pots of them as you dare. They are one of those magical, life-enhancing plants that unfailingly make you beam. The range of varieties is truly mesmerizing and so the next few pages are dedicated to just some of my 'would be lost without' tulips, complete with serving suggestions. One of many praises to sing about tulips is that although they need no accompaniment, they are outstanding team players. It's as if they were created for growing in pots: the marriage of tulip and pot – almost any style of pot – is as harmonious an affiliation as could possibly be.

① Elegant 'Flaming Parrot' is among the last tulips to flower. Here it joins *Iris sibirica* 'Tropic Night' for an eye-popping unison. True blue is the only colour tulips don't stretch to, but this moisture-loving iris obligingly compensates. Its slender swords remain decorative long after the blooms have gone and contrast in form with the bold yellow-margined leaves of *Hosta fortunei* var. *aureomarginata*, which are later joined by spikes of lilac trumpets. *Narcissus* 'Pipit' is a late and long-flowering multi-headed treasure that holds the middle ground.

② Lily-flowered *Tulipa* 'Green Star' rises among rich-blue daisy-flowered *Pericallis* x *hybrida* Senetti Blue as a cool centrepiece. Blue violas form a ring of cheery blooms and, with the senetti, flower into early summer.

③ Hardy perennials and bulbs here achieve a display that has a life beyond the tulips. Blue-green-leaved *Hosta* 'Halcyon' carpets and cushions the rim of the capacious container and up through this shoot grey-green-flowered *Ornithogalum nutans* and *Tulipa* 'Formosa', a viridiflora type with acid-green flowers that contrast superbly with 'Bleu Aimable'. *Camassia leichtlinii* sends its slender stems skyward to burst open its starry blooms as the tulips fade. You can just pick out the tiny white blooms of *Anthriscus sylvestris* 'Ravenswing'. Its feathery, chocolate-brown leaves will later fill out in place of the tulips.

④ This shameless mix of spring-flowering bulbs features heady-scented *Hyacinthus* 'City of Haarlem', saucer-flowered *Anemone coronaria* Harmony Series and short 'Showcase' tulips. Hardy evergreen sedge, *Carex oshimensis* 'Eversheen', fills the gaps and softens the edges.

MORE TULIPS

Far from fleeting in flower, many tulips will last in bloom for an entire month and engagingly alter their composure – and often their colouring – as they age. From the moment the pert buds show a tinge of colour to the fall of the final petal, they'll keep you well entertained. The possible combinations are endless but simplicity usually yields the best effect and so I tend not to use too many varieties in one container. Each of these groups involves no more than three different plants and will still look presentable once the tulips are done.

① 'Apricot Parrot' heads up my chart of the maddest, most characterful and longest flowering of tulips. It is my 'desert island' choice and straight out of an old master painting. Its crinkled, crimped and frilled, multicoloured blooms are eagerly anticipated and appreciated in all its stages over many weeks.

② This flamboyant planting in an oval tin container gushes spring charm. It features some first-rate favourites, including 'Apricot Parrot', that explode from a mound of orange-apricot-leaved Heuchera 'Peach Flambé'. Euphorbia myrsinites extends lax stems clothed in blue-green fleshy leaves and finished off with clusters of acid-green bracts.

3 Ever-obliging heuchera – this one is 'Marmalade' – appears again here as a basal foil to *Tulipa* 'Malaika' ('Bruine Wimpel'), whose glowing bronze blooms are flushed with antique pink. Dainty orange-red-flowered *Geum* 'Flames of Passion' shoots up among the tulips to form a mid-height link. The fresh green leaves of a potted hornbeam provide a lively backdrop.

4 Phormiums (New Zealand flax) look exotic but are surprisingly hardy. For containers, pick compact varieties such as 'Pink Panther'. The splayed petals of lily-flowered *Tulipa* 'Marilyn' display pink stripes that echo the phormium. Variegated ivy forms a trailing base, softening the bucket rim, and *Leptospermum scoparium* 'Martini', another New Zealander, edges in with pink button blooms.

5 *Tulipa* 'Weber's Parrot' and silver-leaved *Brunnera macrophylla* 'Jack Frost' are a great double act, the one a frothy foil to the frilly other. Once the tulips are over, tug them out and shear over the brunnera. Your reward: a fresh flush of perfect leaves.

TULIPSCAPES

Each year I grow as many tulips as possible. I plant a large number as a single variety per pot; this way I don't risk having one variety that is past its best in the same pot as another yet to flower. Tulips lend themselves to mass displays and you can create breathtaking ones by grouping them and raising some on upturned crates, pots or tables. By interspersing them with other plants in season, such as alpines, Japanese maples and spring-flowering perennials, you can realize the most lusciously inviting landscape in the very tightest of spaces.

Ensure potted tulips don't go short of water in the few weeks leading up to flowering. If they are left thirsty, their growth can be seriously stunted.

❶ A trio of my most-relied-upon tulips – red and cream-white 'Grand Perfection', ochre and burgundy 'Gavota' and plum-purple 'Recreado' – join forces with other spring stalwarts. Popped in trays on a wooden bench, the pinks and mauves of *Phlox subulata* 'Candy Stripe', *P. s.* 'Emerald Cushion Blue' and *Saxifraga* 'Peter Pan' sing out against a foil of aromatic French lavenders, *Lavandula* 'Regal Splendour' and *L.* 'Tiara'.

❷ Lit by early morning sun, this scene jumps to life. Repeating the same or tonally similar varieties brings a sense of unity and varying the heights of the containers achieves rhythm and balance. Plentiful leaves offer calm among the tulip mayhem.

❸ There are so many delights in this single scene, I find it completely enthralling. Apart from the exuberant splendour of the tulips themselves, they are bathed in a magical light. They appear to dance. Just a few pots of glamorous tulips (here 'Grand Perfection', 'Caribbean Parrot' and 'Estella Rijnveld') against a leafy backdrop can lift spirits.

IN THE SHADE

Many shade-loving plants are at their best in spring and there are some excellent species to choose from. Ferns and hostas top the list but there are also many other woodland beauties that, unless you have perfect conditions, are more likely to thrive in pots than in the open garden. If you combine foliage and flowers, they will continue to please well beyond spring.

① *Corydalis flexuosa* 'Purple Leaf' bears delicate blooms of brilliant blue that appear to float above the dark foliage.

② Moisture-loving *Hosta* (Tardiana Group) 'Halcyon', perennial forget-me-not *Brunnera macrophylla* 'Looking Glass', ajuga (bugle) and ferns brighten a shady corner in shades of blue. This group will thrive together for a couple of seasons before it is best to separate them. Split each plant and pot some of the healthiest pieces back in the same container with fresh compost.

③ Ferns are a reliable choice for shady containers, whether combined with other perennials and bulbs or annuals and tender perennials to create a lush feel.

④ Mixing soft, delicate material with the big and bold is a guarantee of visual drama. Grown from tubers purchased in early spring, *Sauromatum venosum* (voodoo lily) forms an umbrella-like canopy of dramatic leaves, held on stout, spotted stems and preceded by handsome, but unpleasant-smelling, flowers. Weaving through are *Athyrium filix-femina* 'Frizelliae' – a dainty fern with arching fronds – *Corydalis flexuosa* 'Purple Leaf' and ground-covering, long-flowering *Viola hederacea* (ivy-leaved violet).

⑤ *Dicentra* 'King of Hearts' is a hardy perennial that spreads to form clumps of attractive glaucous leaves and pink locket-shaped blooms produced over a long period. It's a good substitute in, or in addition to, either of the shady planting schemes in ② and ④.

⑥ *Athyrium filix-femina* 'Frizelliae', *Corydalis flexuosa* 'Purple Leaf' and *Viola hederacea* crowd together beneath the huge, fingered leaves of *Sauromatum venosum*, accentuating its striking stems.

47

STARRY BLOOMS

Flowers open in all manner of distinctive shapes from saucers and cups to trumpets and bells. Some face you with their detail, others require you to lift them and peer inside. Star-shaped blooms mostly look straight at you and are in plentiful supply during spring. Here are just a few that twinkle in containers.

① This much-treasured wooden box makes several appearances in the book. It is big enough to contain an impactful display but small enough that it can be inexpensively replanted several times each year. Here, cheery *Viola wittrockiana* 'Ultima Morpho' and *Trifolium repens* 'Atropurpureum' form a carpet, presided over by starry-flowered *Ornithogalum nutans* and, continuing the celestial theme, *Narcissus* 'Baby Moon'.

② Flowering in late April and May and again in late summer, *Clematis* 'Bijou' is a compact cultivar bred especially for containers. Here it partners daisy-flowered *Pericallis* x *hybrida* Senetti Blue for an intense colour pop. Steel-blue *Festuca glauca* 'Intense Blue' sits in an accompanying pot.

③ *Phalaris arundinacea* var. *picta* 'Feesey' is a good-looking but rampant grass I would not let loose in the garden. However, safely contained in an ornamental pot, it has much to offer. Here its stripy leaves are a foil to a pair of ornamental onions, *Allium cristophii* and *A. caeruleum*, bearing round flower heads composed of many stars. Cut the grass down to its base in summer for a surge of fresh foliage but leave the allium spheres for structure.

④ Exotic *Scilla peruviana* is an easy-to-grow spring-flowering bulb with sturdy stems that carry impressive heads of many tiny, starry, sapphire blooms. It's definitely a stand-alone plant, needing no company. Here I've planted three bulbs in a plastic pot and set it into a 'pebblecube' – a wire gabion basket filled with small pebbles and with a central void designed to house a pot.

4

LONG-LASTING PERENNIALS

While many perennials do not flower for long enough or are too tall, invasive or ungainly to be worth growing in pots, there are others that bloom perpetually or have attractive foliage (or both) and so are well suited to pot displays.

1 2 & 3 Planted in April, just starting into growth, this perennial quartet was in full bloom by mid-May and still going strong in late June. Blue-flowered *Polemonium boreale* 'Heavenly Habit' and pink *Dicentra* 'King of Hearts' faded away for the summer, but will return next year, and any gaps were soon filled in by *Geranium* 'Azure Rush' and *Anemone* 'Wild Swan', which bloomed non-stop well into autumn.

4 Tone and texture are key to the effectiveness of this perennial planting, with the wall behind echoing the shades of the leaves. It's subtle but pleasing. Centrally positioned, *Tiarella* 'Pink Skyrocket' produces short spikes of pink buds that open white. *Ajuga reptans* 'Burgundy Glow' is grown primarily for its mottled leaves but also sends up spring spikes of blue flowers. A pair of plum-purple-leaved *Geranium* x *antipodeum* 'Purple Passion' fill out the sides. Cut everything back hard in early summer to reap a new crop of leaves and blooms.

4

PURE AND SIMPLE

Although they can sometimes feel a little over-contrived, carefully thought out colour themes reliably deliver impact, whether from cleverly contrasting shades, a calming blend of harmonious pastels or a single, perhaps favourite, colour. The simplest are the most failsafe – monochromatic whites and silvers always please. Similarly, sticking to either the hot or the cool end of the spectrum usually guarantees colourful success.

① Housed in a sympathetic grey slate trough, *Rhodanthemum* 'Casablanca' creates a dense carpet of silver filigree foliage from which rises a long succession of white daisy-like blooms on grey stems. This superb evergreen often blooms from very early in the season. Either side, *Armeria maritima* 'Alba' ② throws up strong but slender stems topped with pure-white pincushions – snip them off as they fade to keep them blooming. Studded with tiny, brilliant-white saucers, bushy *Arenaria montana* ③ tumbles over the edge, flanking aromatic grey and green variegated *Thymus* 'Silver Posie' ④.

6

5 & **6** This wooden crate is crowded with seed-raised Icelandic poppies (*Papaver nudicaule* Garden Gnome Group) and nothing else. I considered using other plants as well but there is much to be said for the effect attained from pure simplicity. The oranges and the yellows of the papery poppies glow heartwarmingly in the sun, and raising them so they are outlined against blue skies is added joy. You could not do that if they were in a border. Regularly snip off faded flower stems at their base and they will flower for many weeks.

5

SUMMER

SUMMER BULBS

Although not as dominating of the season as their spring counterparts, there are many first-rate summer-flowering bulbs and tubers well suited to growing in pots. The majority bear showy, colourful blooms and among the reliables are gladioli, eucomis, lilies, dwarf dahlias, zantedeschias and begonias. Less commonly planted genera, including polianthes and tigridia, will temporarily augment summer displays.

1 I often plant gladioli to spear up through grasses and perennials. The result is a startling flash of admittedly short-lived but cheering colour. Dwarf and 'butterfly' gladioli perform well in pots, often producing two or three flower stems per corm. Temper their flamboyance with daintier plants, including grasses such as *Panicum virgatum* 'Heavy Metal' (switch grass). Don't cram in too many – less is more in this case – and chop the stems out once they've flowered. Although they will often flower again the following year, for a guaranteed quality display it's sensible to buy new corms annually. Here the narrow blades and airy panicles of the panicum and the bulky blooms of dwarf

Gladiolus 'Flevo Laguna' ② contrast effectively. Eucomis autumnalis subsp. autumnalis (pineapple lily) planted in a ring adds an exotic touch but is frost hardy. The bulbs will produce larger and more plentiful blooms each year. All are attractive in leaf and this combination pleases (albeit on a quieter level) even after flowering.

③ & ④ In my view, many of the shorter lily cultivars, bred primarily for pot culture, are unnaturally stumpy, charmless plants and best avoided. Among the exceptions is 'Sweet Surrender'. At 80–100cm (31½–39½in) it's the optimum height, achieving grace without calling for support. The naturalistic frill of Campanula rotundifolia (common harebell),

Stipa tenuissima, Sisyrinchium 'Biscutella' and Carex comans 'Frosted Curls' anchor them visually and continue to appeal long after the lilies have faded.

⑤ Provided they don't go hungry when in growth or become waterlogged at any point, lilies will thrive in a sufficiently large container for years. Most will bulk up speedily and are best separated and replanted every third year or so. Don't restrict yourself to shorter varieties. Here tall and elegant turk's cap cultivar Lilium 'Claude Shride' (Martagon type) rises from a leafy base of blue-leaved Hosta (Tardiana Group) 'Halcyon'.

PREVIOUS PAGES Displaying fruiting plants and those with tasty leaves or edible flowers among the purely ornamental celebrates the abundance of summer.

SEASIDE

It's possible to create an evocative mood or summon up a distinct feel using just a few appropriately planted pots and accessories. You can be as subtle or as obvious as suits you – that's the joy of it. A seaside theme is easy to pull off. Gather what you think might be useful from a creative foray to a beach or assemble props like driftwood, fossils or weathered rope. It's not necessary to use only plants that suit coastal locations (unless you live by the sea!) – they just need a maritime look. Tufty grasses, hummock-forming perennials and plants with foamy flowers, blue-grey leaves or architectural form (such as palms) are all suitably suggestive.

1 Composed primarily of repeated mounds of foliage, this shore-inspired 'potscape' offers year-round appeal from evergreens, grasses and a restrained embellishment of maritime *objets*. Pale flowers bob over soft foliage on airy, rippling plants such as gaura, while pines, agapanthus and festuca colonize a pebbled base. The 'dotted' positioning of the pots is redolent of the way many true coastal plants grow in relative isolation from each other.

2 With clear blue skies reflected in their high-summer blooms, agapanthus (pictured is 'Lavender Haze') remind us of warm climes and sea views. They are very comfortable in pots, revelling in free-draining compost. They flower best when restricted and, in growth, fed fortnightly with a high-potash fertilizer. Deciduous species are hardier than evergreens.

3 *Isotoma axillaris*, a tender perennial best treated as an annual, is a dependable pot plant. Wiry stems bear a profusion of silvery-blue, starfish-shaped blooms all summer. White- and pink-flowered forms are also available.

4 From this convincing slate-effect trough flows an energetic wave of sun-loving plants. Blue-grey *Euphorbia myrsinites* juts horizontally as if cantilevered; weighted by clusters of lime-green bracts. White *E. hypericifolia* 'Diamond Frost' breaks like flecked surf over the top, while the pink-tinged shell-like bracts of *Origanum* 'Kent Beauty' are echoed in the leaves of sprawling *Hylotelephium sieboldii*. The zingy foliage of *Sedum* 'Lemon Ball' enables an otherwise muted colour scheme to sing.

5 Fleshy, glaucous-leaved *Hylotelephium* 'Thundercloud' tumbles from a pebble-filled gabion-style planter.

6 Very few fuchsias excite me but I would not be without *F. microphylla* subsp. *hemsleyana* 'Silver Lining'. Happy by the coast, superb in pots, silvery leaves, tiny scarlet blooms, purple-black berries and a ground-covering habit – what more can you ask of a little plant?

EXOTIC TOUCH

In summer, many annuals such as nicotiana, amaranthus and ricinus, which look exotic but are not difficult to grow, afford a tropical flavour. It's not necessary to splash out on specimen palms to achieve lushness, although there are several, including trachycarpus, chamaerops, washingtonia, jubaea and cordylines, that excel in pots and are hardy enough to winter outside, calling for fleece and bubble polythene in only the coldest districts and harshest elemental conditions. In my experience, one to avoid is *Phoenix canariensis* (Canary Island date palm): it's too wide, too fast and too sharp. Whether you invest in permanent 'tropicals' or not depends on your fondness for them: I have very few. In terms of other plants, bold handsome leaves, a lively growth rate and startlingly coloured flowers are all desirable characteristics for an eye-challenging result. Calm your display – if you prefer – by adding in contrasting softer material, such as grasses and plants with tiny leaves.

1 Glamorous-looking *Eucomis comosa* is surprisingly hardy and easy to grow. In winter, move pots to a shed or garage to keep bulbs dry.

2 *Musa acuminata* 'Dwarf Cavendish', a compact ornamental banana cultivar ideal for pots.

3 From dormant tubers to towering columns of bold stripey leaves in a matter of weeks, *Canna* 'Phasion' adds drama to any display.

4 This attention-grabbing quartet focuses on big leaves and intense, saturated shades. Like many plantings themed to the 'exotic', it makes a sizeable statement, requiring a container 60cm (24in) plus, deep and wide. Rhizomatous *Canna* 'Phasion' shoots up in a variegated blaze to 1.5m (5ft) or more. Reflecting its colouring, *Solenostemon scutellarioides* 'Sunset Boulevard' (coleus) is of more modest stature and nestles in front of intensely coloured *Dahlia* 'Karma Choc'. *Eucomis bicolour* (pineapple lily) completes with strap-shaped leaves and tufted blooms on sturdy stems.

5 Not every container we plant needs be serious. Best described as a semi-controlled explosion, this wacky planting is a bit of frivolous botanical fun. At its centre, handsome banana-relative *Musa acuminata* 'Dwarf Cavendish' forms a slowly expanding, living sculpture. 'Buggy', a dwarf gladiolus, amuses with a splay of temporary flamboyance. Its pale-yellow 'eyes' reflect the sculpted foliage of *Ipomoea batatas* 'Bright Ideas Lime' (sweet potato vine), while low but bushy pink-flowered *Cuphea hyssopifolia* (false heather) contrasts. Prune out the expendable gladioli after flowering and let the banana take up dominance.

EDIBLE AND VISUAL

Opportunity to grow fresh, flavoursome, chemically unsullied food floats many a gardening obsession. Whether an entire meal or just a few leaves, it's always a thrill when homegrown meets plate. An extensive range of produce can readily be grown in pots literally on your doorstep. It's the wonderful duality of tasty edibility and ornamental good looks that leads me to give over so many of my summer containers to productive plants.

1 This wooden drawer was inexpensively procured from a closing-down junk shop – it screamed 'plant me!' Containers of these proportions are ideal for fast-developing but compact crops, such as lettuce, rocket, mustard, leaf beet, oriental greens and other highly nutritious snip-and-come-again baby leaves. It has a large surface area but is not too deep. Line with polythene and drill plenty of holes in the base for drainage, to lengthen the life of the wood. Fill with good-quality soilless compost and scatter seeds directly. In spring and summer germination takes just a few days. Once the crop is exhausted, tip out and repeat the process.

❷ Same drawer, different contents. The talents of a nasturtium (*Tropaeolum majus*) are many and they are the easiest plant to grow, especially in pots of poor, shallow compost (a child can do it). Pickling the seed pods, tossing the flowers in a salad and chewing the raw earthy, mustard-flavoured leaves are all options; their edible parts can also be combined with chillies and whipped into a fiery sauce. They are beloved of bees. Simply paired with another easy, edible-petalled annual, calendula (pot or English marigold), they glow like beacons on even the most overcast occasions.

❸ In containers, dwarf bush and trailing or tumbling tomatoes will produce heavy crops. 'Tumbling Tom Yellow' offers masses of highly ornamental yellow cherry fruits.

❹ Not every plant here can be eaten but there's no reason not to mix the edible with the purely aesthetic to enrich the visual effect. Gathered here are plants that will endure all summer, rather than those that will peter out part way. Exceptions are the sunflowers (*Helianthus annuus* 'Little Leo'): sow them at intervals for a succession of irrepressible blooms. The overall freshness and vibrancy comes both from healthy plants – yellowing foliage and straggly growth will always detract – and from balancing bursts of colour with quieter greens. The varying shapes and textures and the raising up of key plants, such as cascading tomatoes ('Tumbling Tom Red') and purple-fruited aubergines ('Baby Rosanna'), to ensure their containers are visible, contribute to the liveliness. Saved from recycling, the olive oil tins have lasted several years and are my first-choice homes for peppers, tomatoes and aubergines.

5 Tin cans are useful for raising seedlings and growing on, but drill plenty of holes in the base before filling with compost and sowing. Basil is a very useful herb that I enjoy having to hand for as much of the year as possible. It is easily raised from seed but doesn't suit being planted in a mixed pot as it resents being too wet or crowded by other plants. Sow direct into a larger tin and it will live out its aromatic life without need for transplanting.

6 Pea flowers (from edible *Pisum sativum*) are as pretty as any you could wish for. Do not confuse with sweet peas (*Lathyrus odoratus*), which are poisonous.

7 As well as bearing delicious fruits, courgette plants supply visual drama, courtesy of their handsome marbled leaves and large golden-yellow blooms. Interspersing with nasturtiums shades their thirsty roots.

As long as they don't go short of moisture, courgettes grow well in large containers. For greater ornamental appeal, choose a yellow-fruited variety. The edible blooms can be fried, stuffed or added to salads.

8 Even in full growth, this large wooden crate, once used to transport paving slabs, could conceivably be shifted on a pallet truck so qualifies as a container, despite having the proportions of a raised bed. Similar crates can be obtained cheaply or for nothing. When lined with polythene or pond liner and filled with a mix of garden soil and compost, they offer exciting scope for an impressive display of sizeable plants. Their rustic appearance and capaciousness particularly suit fast growing edibles: here yellow courgettes, dwarf runner beans, nasturtiums and peas.

⑨ Brought together in this wide terracotta container as young plants in mid-spring, this carefully chosen collection of herbs should amiably cohabit all summer. Separate the plants at the end of summer, by which time they'll be congested. Blue and pink hyssop (*Hyssopus officinalis* and *H. o.* 'Roseus'), dill (*Anethum graveolens*) and Russian tarragon (*Artemisia dracunculus* var. *inodora*) all rise elegantly. Salad burnet (*Sanguisorba minor*), chives (*Allium schoenoprasum*), strawberry mint (*Mentha* x *piperita* 'Strawberry') and dwarf French lavenders (*Lavandula stoechas* Javelin Series) bush out.

⑩ Many herbs grow rapidly and are best kept apart from each other for manageability. Mints are a classic. Plant them in a mixed pot – or a border or raised bed – and they'll run. An attractive method of keeping herbs together but separated is to pot them individually and then plunge them side by side in a much larger container, partially filled with free-draining compost. Then, when any become pot bound, overgrown or are on the brink of escape, you can whip them out and replace them with others on standby. An old tin bath is sympathetically fit for purpose and here houses my collection of thymes, potted into terracotta, then arranged at differing heights to accentuate each. The principle works for any herbs, bringing them nearer to eye and nostril, and in an orderly fashion that makes them easier to care for.

ADD WATER

In feature form, water endows a garden with an engaging extra dimension. Using a container, you can comfortably bring the life-enhancing qualities of water, as well as some of the enthralling fauna it attracts and supports, where there isn't room for a pond proper. This can be as simple as a shallow, reflective steel bowl or a more elaborate potted pool or fountain. In my view, water features usually show best when set mainly among foliage, rather than excessively flowery plants.

1 A vintage galvanized tank is an ideal choice for a water feature. Pygmy waterlilies will live happily in a pond of this size but will take a while to bulk up. The easiest and most instantly impactful option, although often not frost hardy, is floating plants such as bright green, foam-textured *Pistia stratiotes* (water lettuce) and *Salvinia natans*, an aquatic fern, which will provide summer shade, reducing algal growth and green water. *Juncus effusis* f. *spiralis* (corkscrew rush) is at home in shallow water and strikingly contrasts the floating aquatics.

2 A 'bog' pot goes some distance towards sating those who love lush, moisture-craving plants but garden on a dry soil. I've had that issue all my gardening life so here I've lined a terracotta pot with polythene and restricted the drainage hole with a small stone, before filling with a 50:50 mix of loam and soilless compost. Once planted, it requires very little attention other than watering. There are many excellent damp lovers – some rather too sizeable to sustain in the average pot – so this selection is necessarily conservative. Allowed to mingle, *Hosta* 'Patriot', feathery *Astilbe* 'Bronce Elegans' (*simplicifolia* hybrid), *Imperata cylindrica* 'Rubra' and stately zantedeschias span many months with blooms and handsome foliage. Keep these plants considerably less wet during winter.

3 Even a small body of water can attract dragonflies, although usually only in passing as they hunt for insect prey. They are fascinating creatures, exquisite in their detail, and it's a thrill whenever they rest in my presence. This female common darter tarried a while.

1

4 This twee but entertaining fountain consists of a large galvanized container, a small submersible pump that sits in the bottom and coloured bottles. Push the pump lead through a drainage hole and secure with silicone sealant. Stand the bottles on heavy-duty galvanized mesh, in turn supported on an upturned bottomless plastic bucket. A pipe from the pump is pushed through a hole in the central bottle, drilled carefully using a tile drill bit. Top up regularly when in use. Ditch the bottles for a less fussy self-contained water feature.

BOXES OF COLOUR & TEXTURE

Wooden crates have great visual and nostalgic appeal. They are of a shape and size not available in many other materials, yet in those respects I find them perfect containers. Mine are precious, so to extend their life as planters they are emptied and brought under cover in winter. Painting the insides with wood preservative, lining with polythene and raising off the ground to aid drainage also keep them in service for as long as possible. Most of mine are genuinely pre-used but as the oldest of them inevitably disintegrate, they are replaced with readily available replicas that weather convincingly in a single season.

❶ This box of sun-loving perennials strikes multi-season interest. In early summer the papery pink blooms of *Geranium sanguineum* var. *striatum* 'Splendens' open in quick succession as *Hylotelephium telephium* (Atropurpureum Group) 'Purple Emperor' and *H.* 'Carl' rise and bud up. In the centre, *Salvia* x *superba* sends up spikes of blue that are later cut down to allow the hylotelephiums to reign.

❷ The tight buds of *Hylotelephium* 'Carl' open as a late summer mass of myriad pink stars that are favoured by bees and butterflies.

❸ Although its flowers become less plentiful, the handsome-leaved geranium continues its sprawl through the hylotelephiums well into autumn, realizing an engaging scramble of textures. As they age, the hylotelephium flowers redden, then rust in dignified autumnal demise. Leave them intact for winter structure – they are enchanting dusted in hoar frost or snow.

❹ This 'copy' crate sited in full sun hosts intermingling tiers of *Capsicum annuum* 'Chenzo' (chilli pepper), speared through by supremely elegant, lamp-like *Bessera elegans* (coral drops). A drape of contrasting foliage comes courtesy of *Origanum vulgare* 'Country Cream' (a variegated oregano), *Lysimachia congestiflora* 'Midnight Sun' and *Thymus* 'Hartington Silver'. It's brimming with colour and texture, invitingly tactile and even edible in parts. And I love the shadows thrown by the trailing stems.

❺ This informal assembly of sun-worshipping *Verbena* 'Lollipop' (a shorter version of *V. bonariensis* more gainly for containers), trailing pink-flowered calibrachoa and cherry-fruited Tomato 'Tumbler' is knitted together by a froth of starry-flowered *Isotoma axillaris* to create a long-lasting display. A large wooden crate provides them with plenty of growing space so each reaches full potential.

SUMMER PROFUSION

Midsummer in the garden is a time of excited collision. There's so much activity as to be an overwhelming – but oh, so welcome! – assault on our senses. Every available pot is planted and, after a surge of growth, helped along by warmth, watering and a drop of fertilizer, they are full to bursting. There's a danger of floral overload from what are loosely termed 'bedding' and 'patio' plants. I believe you can have too many flowers and sometimes less really is more. Ensure there's plenty of calming and contrasting foliage, both coloured and more muted and neutral. Narrow your plantings down by choosing a theme, fulfilling a purpose or paying homage to an inspirational image you've seen.

1 For me, summer is a time when the more pots, the merrier. That doesn't mean legions of tiny pots that dry out as soon as you turn your back, rather those of 30cm (12in) diameter minimum, with many considerably larger. Having a range of plants individually potted gives opportunity to shake up the display and change the look as the season progresses. Clustered together they will create a protected microclimate, the larger specimens serving to shelter the smaller. In this garden, on the concreted site of an old stable yard, there was not even the tiniest pocket of soil. Two choices: drill and dig for weeks, fill skips and import topsoil, or grow in pots. No contest! Painted in a neutral shade and softened by potted plants that rise to meet it, the greenhouse is integral to the scene.

2 Individually potted heuchera, argyranthemum, pelargonium, phormium and solenostemon (coleus) here create a tapestry of flowers and foliage that is easy to reconfigure and expand or shrink.

3 Set in a muted landscape of mint greens and soft textures, this is a strong planting of starkly contrasting dark and light, very gently warmed by terracotta and the neutral environs. If set with other more colourfully planted containers, its impact would be so diminished as to be wasted. There's plenty more growing to go on here. Tender perennials *Petunia* Designer Cappuccino and *P.* Happy Magic Charcoal Black are bolstered by evergreen *Hebe* 'Lady Ann' and an ebony trail of *Ipomoea batatas* 'Sidekick Black Heart'.

4 A pared-back palette of white, steely-blue and champagne gold lends this trio of pots a sophisticated air, whilst the varying heights and styles of container are playful. Behind, a white form of *Lycianthes* (formerly *Solanum*) *rantonettii* is underplanted with *Euphorbia hypericifolia* 'Diamond Frost'. In front, semi-evergreen *Abelia* x *grandiflora* 'Hopleys' flows from a slender bucket and *Festuca glauca* 'Intense Blue' (blue fescue) co-ordinates with its patterned pot.

5 Where shade reigns for most or all of the day, ferns and begonias revel. The juxtaposition of bright and floriferous begonia with feathery copper shield fern (*Dryopteris erythrosora*) – a reliable favourite – set against the dark, handsome swords of *Phormium* 'Chocomint' makes for a stimulating visual effect. Phormiums (New Zealand flax) are surprisingly tolerant of shade and can be divided in spring if they become too large.

6 Often it is most effective to plant containers with a single variety. It's a low-risk strategy that allows for grouping and rearranging of pots to create associations that might not work practically if those plants were housed together in the same container. Singling out varieties also encourages you to appreciate them more closely. Petunias are often rejected by horticultural snobs but many recent introductions, such as *P.* Happy Magic Dark Caramel Star (pictured), are interestingly shaded and team agreeably with weathered terracotta.

7 The blue-grey foliage of evergreen *Eucalyptus gunnii* and heart-shaped, silver-adorned burgundy leaves of *Persicaria microcephala* 'Red Dragon' (knotweed) set off *Petunia* Phantom perfectly. The latter's unusual yellow and near black striped blooms can be hard to place but here it brings a sense of fun and is calmed by its companions.

8 Bamboo pipes are ideal for injecting height among standard collections of containers and especially suit succulents which deserve elevation to showcase their sculptural elegance. These fleshy-leaved plants are a gift to haphazard gardeners who have little time to water (or forget to), although even these supremely drought-tolerant plants get thirsty eventually and need watering occasionally. Thriving here are *Echeveria* 'Perle von Nürnberg', *Sedum* 'Lemon Ball', *Sempervivum calcareum* and *E. runyonii* 'Topsy Turvy' (its waxy, silvery-grey leaves are rolled downwards along their length, and then curled up at the tips).

9 This may look like an unconsidered jumble – and to a degree it is because no great effort has gone into arranging them – but the assortment of colours, textures and shapes and, importantly, their loose repetition bounces the eye in excited exploration. Calming green mounds temper the lively pops of colour, whilst daintier flowers and foliage provide coherence. Offer the human eye plenty to feast on and it will. This is a haphazard yet balanced scene that keeps me engaged even though I see it every day. There's always a fresh focus and a few moments spent rearranging and tinkering are a therapeutic start or end to any day.

6

7

8

SUMMER PERENNIALS

Industrious perennials that flower continually or repeatedly for many months, or additionally bear colourful or sculptural foliage, are generally exemplary container candidates, even if, due to their energetic growth, they will only go one season before they require separating and planting out or repotting. Grasses, shrubbier perennials and subshrubs are included in this group. Bolster them with tender perennials, shrubs, bulbs and annuals for a hard-working, season-spanning display.

❶ The jaunty angles of this flamboyant entanglement of wiry perennials add to its charm. Shrubby, silver-leaved *Teucrium fruticans* 'Compactum' threads through and effectively marries two vibrant but very different salvias: red-flowered 'Royal Bumble' and purple 'Amistad'. *Glandularia* (formerly *Verbena*) Temari Patio Blue picks up the intense purple to anchor and unify. Similarly tasked is the red argyranthemum in the foreground below.

Position in a sunny, sheltered corner and prune judiciously to prevent plants becoming too ungainly.

2 *Salvia* 'Amistad' is among the most constantly in flower of all perennials.

3 Verbena and pennisetum are enchantingly highlighted on a sunny summer eve.

4 In a large pot *Persicaria amplexicaulis* 'JS Delgado Macho' will push through other long-flowering perennials to create a relaxed jostle.

5 If sited to take advantage of light, tall grasses and airy perennials, such as stalwart *Verbena bonariensis*, can be magically illuminated. When these plants are backlit or, more gently, side lit, the effect can be spectacular. In summer, it is at sunrise and sunset, when the sun is lower, that this is most successful. You can shunt pots around and raise them until you've found the optimum light spot. Pennisetums (here *P. macrourum*, and *P. setaceum* 'Sky Rocket') are especially fit for purpose, their feathery plumes held proud to catch the light. Snip *Eucalyptus gunnii* regularly to keep it in check. Mine is massacred each late November to make my Christmas door wreath, and both coppiced and root pruned in spring. A couple of large *Carex* 'Milk Chocolate' plants, split into several, act as a bronze ruff.

6 No apologies here for drafting in another salvia ('Wendy's Wish') or more fountain grasses *(Pennisetum setaceum* 'Fireworks') – both are accomplished container plants. Also composing this concoction of pink and claret shades is a couple of reliable knotweeds: tall *Persicaria amplexicaulis* and shorter *P. a.* 'JS Delgado Macho'. Weaving around below is diminutive *Fuchsia microphylla* subsp. *hemsleyana* 'Silver Lining'. They'll all be clamouring for release by the end of the season but that is after months of loyal service. Let them die down naturally, providing skeletal winter structure, then separate and replant in early spring. Treat the pennisetum as an annual, divide the persicaria and prune the salvia hard.

7 Intermingled in a large pot, *Persicaria amplexicaulis*, *Pennisetum setaceum* 'Fireworks' (fountain grass) and *Scabiosa atropurpurea* 'Blackberry Scoop' forge a sumptuous, long-lasting alliance.

DAZZLING DAISIES

Daisies (*Asteraceae/Compositae*) are one of the largest plant families on the planet. You could fill a whole garden with these flowers and not be bored. Many, including a number of tender perennials mainly native to Africa, are ideal container plants, due to their extended flowering period and bushy stature. Plant breeders work tirelessly on them, widening the colour range and improving performance. Single flowers are preferable to doubles, as they are more useful to pollinators.

1 Crowded with bright-yellow, cone-centred blooms, *Rudbeckia fulgida* 'Little Goldstar' is a sun-loving hardy perennial that duets here with *Helichrysum petiolare* 'Limelight', a half-hardy trailing plant with pale-lemon foliage. The dark lead-effect trough accentuates the leaves and, raised on an old sewing machine stand, magnifies the impact of this simple scheme. A fountain of creamy-white *Phalaris arundinacea* var. *picta* 'Feesey' is balanced in the foreground by *Phormium cookianum* subsp. *hookeri* 'Cream Delight'. Lemon osteospermums pick up the theme.

2 *Erigeron karvinskianus*, a self-seeding, ground-covering gem of a perennial that flowers from spring until autumn, is at its best flowing from a tall pot.

3 Prized for its true-blue blooms, *Felicia amelloides* (kingfisher daisy) is an obliging tender perennial, thriving in full sun and

bearing a constant supply of yellow-centred daisies, held well above the leaves on wiry stems. Treat them gently because branches snap readily (I've often accidentally been left with half a plant)!

④ Hailing originally from South Africa, osteospermums are available in a constantly increasing variety of delicious shades and bicolours.

⑤ While a downpour leaves some blooms looking bedraggled, others, including many daisies, wear the drops with style. *Argyranthemum* 'Starlight Red' (Daisy Crazy Series) appears more intense after a shower and sparkles on those uplifting occasions when the sun promptly reappears.

⑥ Displaying several plants of the same type or flower form together can visually be very successful. If nothing else, you get to understand the amazing variety within a single genus or family. I think this abundance of daisy-flowered plants, including argyranthemum, osteospermum, felicia and erigeron, achieves a charming synergy. I love the variety of flower sizes, heights, habits and shades shown in close relation to each other. There's no colour theme; it is intentionally busy and jewel-box-like. Spires of persicaria in the distance and a raised pot of chilli peppers provide just enough relief in this otherwise daisy monopoly.

TABLE TOPS

Many intriguing but tiny plants can be fully appreciated only if raised up and brought to the fore in pots. My own garden features oft-rearranged and ever-expanding collections elevated on a variety of makeshift platforms (see *Raise them up*, page 31). Their scale makes them satisfyingly manageable to create and look after – and they always provoke favourable comment. (see *Tiny plants*, page 124). Elevating a group of small plants of varying shapes, foliage patterns and surfaces to a height that eliminates bending allows you to appreciate them more comfortably and in brilliant close up. There is much to enjoy in the detail.

1 Standing out from the crowd on my trusty upturned dustbin, Aeonium 'Velour' makes a striking but simple centrepiece. At this height you get a better sense of its architectural form than if it were on the ground. It sits in a scape of soft textures that emphasizes its density.

2 This colour-calm but form- and texture-lively arrangement contrasts lush, alien-looking, insectivorous *Sarracenia leucophylla* and *S. x moorei* with angular succulent *Echeveria lilacina* and *Sempervivum calcareum*. The succulents need little water, while the moisture-loving insect devourers sit in saucers regularly topped up from the practically and ornamentally located glass bottles. Age-enhanced terracotta and feathery-leaved cushions of *Leptinella squalida* 'Platt's Black' and *Drosera capensis* (Cape sundew) complete this tactile miniscape.

3 In order to keep them neatly separated for ease of repotting, but also displaying them close together for effect, these Lilliputian foliage plants are potted individually, then grouped in a vintage enamelled bowl. Jauntiness comes from mixing planted pots with empty ones and stacking some while tilting others. It's easy to shift the whole lot without disturbing the contents and also to replace individual plants as necessary.

4 There's no reason not to display plants and objects outdoors in the same way you might in your living room, especially when they are close by a window or paved area. Just a modest, restrained collection arranged on a simple table can inexpensively enliven a dull corner and, using the right plants, will demand very little care. The rhythmic undulation and juxtaposition of shapes and textures here thrills the eye and invites therapeutic stroking, caressing and patting (excepting of the cactus, of course!). *Aloe aristata*, *Sisyrinchium* 'E. K. Balls', *Kalanchoe delagoensis*, *Acaena microphylla* 'Kupferteppich' (syn. *A. m.* 'Copper Carpet'), *Echinocactus grusonii* (golden barrel cactus), echeveria and *Leucophyta brownii* sit on a slab of marble, supported by a repurposed sewing-machine base. Perfectly placed, an ammonite and a clock found in a junk shop raise the visual appeal.

WALL POTS

Hanging baskets are omitted from this book simply because they don't fit my aesthetic. Wall pots are a different story. They present a charming way to adorn vertical surfaces and greet the eye level. Most are not capacious and so are best suited to plants with small root systems, such as succulents and alpine plants, or replanted every few months.

1 Drain hoppers and (well-secured) antique cisterns make for playful wall planters, especially those that display historic layers of peeling paint. Here the revealed colours perfectly complement *Libertia ixioides* 'Taupo Blaze', an evergreen perennial composed of orange, green and bronze leaves arranged in fans. Fixed to a characterful chunk of weathered timber, it provides vertical accent wherever called for. In the foreground is *Pelargonium* 'Vancouver Centennial'.

2 Just one trailing begonia will more than fill the average wall pot and that's how I think they look best: singled out. In pots placed on the ground their cascading habit can be wasted but on a wall they can be positioned at optimum viewing level. Their blooms are far too showy for me to allow more than one or two into my garden. That said, they can bring much-needed colour to shady walls and, if employed sparingly and tempered by subtle foliage, they are of value.

3 'Green' or living walls are increasingly seen on commercial buildings in major cities and at their best can be very effective. This eccentric live-wall feature is as close to one as I'll ever plant and is more appropriate for domestic settings. It displays the definition, texture, contrast and charisma of which an unbroken wall of green is bereft. Old drain hoppers spill with handsome-leaved *Dianella tasmanica*, *Ophiopogon planiscapus* 'Nigrescens' and grassy *Hakonechloa macra*, which becomes entertainingly animated in the slightest breeze. These are fluffed up with coral-flowered *Bessera elegans* and frothy *Euphorbia hypericifolia* 'Diamond Frost'. A rusty manhole surround frames them.

4 Ebony-leaved *Ophiopogon planiscapus* 'Nigrescens' often bears jet-coloured berries, here set off by the fresh-green blades of *Hakonechloa macra*. Planted as dry bulbs in spring, *Bessera elegans* pops up through the grass, opening its long-lasting orange-red blooms in midsummer.

5 My shaded old shed was quickly elevated from eyesore to eye candy, thanks to some careful pot positioning and rustic garb in the form of decommissioned work tools. In cool, dark spots, ferns excel and, provided they receive enough water, thrive in containers. Wicker isn't the most durable material but will last a few years. Planted with ferns, it is visually sympathetic and, hung on the shed, these cone-shaped planters present the fronds near perfectly.

QUICK CLIMBERS

Treated as annuals, many fast-maturing, tender climbing plants inexpensively and relatively speedily deliver both height and drama. They are particularly useful in new gardens and also in smaller plots because they take up very little ground space. Most excel in containers, flowering until late in the year.

❶ Two plants each of *Ipomoea purpurea* 'Grandpa Otts' and *Thunbergia* 'Orange Wonder', scrambling over an arch of lime branches, are the centrepiece of this 'island', designed to be viewed from all angles. The ipomoea presents a fresh batch of trumpet blooms each day but, as its common name of morning glory implies, they weary by noon. To catch them freshly unfurled is reason enough to get up early. Late in the season thunbergia dominates as the

ipomoea peters out and concentrates on producing seed for next year. Augmenting pots include scented sweet peas (*Lathyrus odoratus* 'Matucana'), daisy-flowered *Rudbeckia* Summerina Series and *Euonymus fortunei* 'Kewensis'.

2 As a rule, 'annual' climbing plants come into their own in the latter half of summer. Through September both *Ipomoea lobata* and *Thunbergia* 'Orange Wonder' – a favourite pairing – flowered increasingly profusely, a remarkable performance in a pot 45cm (18in) square by 60cm (24in) high, watered thoroughly every other day and liquid fed fortnightly. Planted in a trough, this duo will create an impressive temporary screen. Behind, trumpet-flowered *Ipomoea tricolor* 'Heavenly Blue' scrambles through a groaning honeysuckle (lonicera).

3 *Rhodochiton atrosanguineum* (purple bell vine) is a tender perennial that prefers slightly cooler, shadier conditions and should ideally be trained on hoops or along horizontals to allow its 'bells' to dangle and dance freely.

4 *Ipomoea lobata* (Spanish flag) is easy to grow from seed and stunning when illuminated.

5 My soil is not suited to sweet peas (*Lathyrus odoratus*) and they are not the easiest plants to keep going in containers. However, their perfume is so vital an ingredient of summer that a high maintenance, slightly compromised potful is infinitely preferable to no sweet peas at all.

6 Cardinal climber (*Ipomoea x multifida*) is dainty of structure but strong in colour and adept at scrambling through shrubs and tall perennials.

7 Not all climbers are desperate to climb. Many, including thunbergias (here *T.* 'Arizona Glow'), are happy trailing, or even as ground cover. This is a single plant in a 25cm (10in) diameter pot, sitting in a chimney pot. Fortnightly liquid feeding and regular thorough watering kept it in prime condition for five months. Contrast of shape is supplied by the *Phormium cookianum* subsp. *hookeri* 'Cream Delight'.

SUMMER SCENTS

Among the plentiful joys of growing in containers is that you can bring the best of the season as near as you wish when it's at its peak. This includes locating fragrant and aromatic plants at the heart of seating areas, on tables, alongside paths and immediately outside doors and windows. The trick is to balance multiple scents and avoid an olfactory overload.

❶ Sun-loving, sugar-pink-flowered *Nemesia denticulata* (syn. *N.* 'Confetti') offers up a tireless supply of sweet, air-pervading perfume from late spring until the frosts. It is especially potent on warm days. Nemesias come in many colours but not all are scented, so sniff before you buy. Accompanying here are trailing silver-leaf *Helichrysum petiolare* 'Microphyllum', perennial *Trifolium repens* 'Dragon's Blood' and mini petunia-like *Calibrachoa* 'Chameleon Pink Passion'.

❷ Chosen for their non-lingering, non-clashing perfume, each of the plants composing this cottage-garden-style arrangement invites close inspection to sample their individual scent. White-flowered *Dianthus* 'Memories' (garden pink) bears the strongest fragrance here. Next in potency is cherry pie-scented heliotrope (*Heliotropium arborescens* 'Marino Blue'), while the repeated lavenders (*Lavandula stoechas* 'Javelin Blue') and tricolour sage (*Salvia officinalis* 'Tricolor') release their respective aromas on touch. Unscented *Glandularia* (formerly *Verbena*) Lanai® Vintage Vodka serves to blend and unify.

❸ Scented-leaf pelargoniums flourish in containers – terracotta shows them off advantageously. Some are shy flowerers but all bear handsome leaves that, when tickled, release an aroma that ranges, depending on variety, from lemon through strawberry and cola to the slightly nutty spiciness of 'Shottesham Pet' (pictured).

❹ On sun-warmed days, the many purple blooms of heliotrope smell unmistakably of cooked cherries. They are among my summer essentials. Occasionally you'll catch a waft but more likely a bit of nose pressing is required, so raise them up in a tall pot for ease. Pictured is *Heliotropium arborescens* 'Marino Blue'.

❺ Compact cultivars of lavender make exemplary, if short-lived, container plants for a sun-baked spot. Those of French lavender (cultivars of *Lavandula stoechas*) are particularly attractive in flower and leaf, and pleasingly pungent when handled.

❻ Of all the delicious perfumes that help compose a perfect summer, honeysuckle is the one I'd take to my desert island. It's part nostalgia, reminding me of gardens and summer evenings from my childhood, as well as the wild woodbine (*Lonicera periclymenum*) hedgerows I stalked in pursuit of butterflies. And so here's first-rate *L. p.* 'Scentsation', captured and tamed in a pot and sited in an evening sun trap. I head there at the close of almost every day: the fragrance is intoxicating and the experience detoxing and de-stressing. Pine-scented *Pelargonium* Fragrans Group, spicy *P.* 'Shottesham Pet' and common thyme (*Thymus vulgaris*) all call for a little stroking to release their respective aromas and so can be enjoyed without taint to the honeysuckle.

AUTUMN

COOLING DOWN

In early autumn, the combination of falling temperatures and steadily reducing daylight hours slows growth and thins flowers, and there's a distinct feeling of change in the air. Many summer plants will bloom on for weeks but a sudden frost can halt them completely, so it's wise to have some resilient autumnal plantings lined up to take over. These may be a single species per pot – perhaps just a cushion chrysanthemum, violas or autumn crocus – to sit among summer survivors, or crisp, unfussy arrangements that capture this most atmospheric of seasons.

PREVIOUS PAGES Autumn is a vibrant, fast-moving season. Flowers come and go, whilst leaves colour up and fall, and fruits ripen. This seasonal offering includes summer lingerers and will continue until temperatures drop away.

① Supported by the curiously wiggly leaves of *Juncus effusus* f. *spiralis* (corkscrew rush) the elegant goblets of *Crocus speciosus* 'Conqueror' open on warm days, showing off their intricate detail. Autumn-flowering crocus seem more robust than those of spring, yet are sadly underrated; planted at the end of summer they'll bloom within weeks. Irresistible for their rich-blue trumpets, gentians (here *Gentiana scabra* 'Rocky Diamond Blue') are lost in the garden unless given a pocket of fibrous, humus-rich soil on a rock garden or, more easily, potted and moved within comfortable view.

② Using a trio of plants with contrasting habits and textures that are unified by colour is an easy and reliable planting format. *Calluna vulgaris* 'Alexandra' (bud-blooming heather) supplies height and featheriness, while the bulky ornamental cabbage is loosely echoed by the silvery-leaved, mauve-flowered cyclamens.

③ This old brick is one of my smallest, yet most often replanted, containers. Here it is stuffed with *Viola* 'Sorbet Antique Shade', which will bloom profusely through autumn and during mild spells in winter.

④ *Saxifraga* 'Rubrifolia' (*fortunei*) is an excellent late flowerer, very at home in a pot. On bright days and in a gentle breeze, its spidery, pure-white blooms literally sparkle. Tucked behind, *Dianthus barbatus* 'Dash Crimson' bears blood-red blooms that add depth and are picked up in the iron-coloured stems and leaf undersides of the saxifrage. Frilly-petalled, half-hardy cyclamens ('Super Serie Petticoat') can be enjoyed indoors later in the season.

⑤ An elegant container, taller than wide, accentuates the wiry verticals of evergreen *Corokia* x *virgata* 'Red Wonder' and wispy red-tinted *Panicum virgatum* 'Squaw'. Tender perennial *Isotoma axillaris* continues its burst of starry blooms as long as temperatures hold up, while claret-leaved *Pennisetum purpureum* 'Princess', a non-flowering cultivar, adds substance.

MELLOWNESS & MAGICAL LIGHT

Once fully aware of how much softer, more diffused and atmospheric is the light of autumn compared to that of summer, you will spot many thrilling effects and enjoy siting plants to take advantage. In pots, they can be raised up or moved around to find the best light-harnessing positions. Papery blooms and colouring leaves are highlighted by slanting rays and turned to stained glass when dramatically backlit. Translucent seed heads appear gilded and the low-level sun casts long, dramatic shadows.

❶ Encircling an upright-growing plant with shorter, more lax varieties is an effective and easy-to-translate container formula, especially using combinations of perennials and grasses for a lengthy display. The mutually flattering perennials here are well matched to their pot and bolstered by the backdrop of a weathered wooden door. Come September, *Coreopsis verticillata* 'Moonbeam' is a mass of palest yellow blooms that gleam in kindly light. Deliberate streaks in the pot's glaze appear to reflect the slender leaves of *Uncinia rubra* 'Belinda's Find', while the timber background echoes their colouring.

❷ Although fleeting, the unusual purple berries of *Callicarpa bodinieri* var. *giraldii* 'Profusion' are a surefire talking point. They glisten in the soft light. Their clustered arrangement and colouring are mirrored in the blooms of *Verbena rigida* in this informal assembly of late-interest perennials that includes *Heucheras* 'Shanghai'. Shell-pink *Hesperantha coccinea* 'Wilfred H. Bryant' and luminous mauve *Tradescantia* (Andersoniana Group) 'Iris Prichard' flower at differing heights so as not to obscure each other. The gaps between these plants are key to the success of the overall visual: effect: once overcrowded, the effect is lost and that's the time to start over.

❸ When the sun sinks directly behind them, the saucer-shaped blooms of *Hesperantha coccinea* 'Oregon Sunset' are transformed. Raising them well above ground in a pot affords them a greater chance of catching the light.

❹ *Pennisetum alopecuroides* 'Cassian's Choice' is among the finest of these obligingly easy and useful mid-height perennial grasses. The wispy late-summer flowers give way to fluffy seed heads that last through winter.

❺ Planted in spring with a jumble of young grasses and perennials for a semi-naturalistic look, this commodious, scrounged crate was quickly a billowing mass of leaf and bloom that continued throughout autumn. For this effect, choose airy or feathery perennials, such as gaura, persicaria and veronicastrum, that won't drown out the grasses. This planting appeared especially magical on misty mornings, as well as on even damper occasions, when rain dripped from bloom to leaf and leaf to bloom.

FRUITS & BERRIES

The harvest season presents its bounty in an extensive range of shapes, sizes and shades from edible apples and quinces to hedgerow hips and clustered berries, borne by plants of every scale. Among them are many admirable container plants, especially those that also offer attractive flowers and/or foliage, such as berberis, cotoneaster, euonymus and vaccinium (blueberries). Berries are an essential garden ingredient at this time, both for our enjoyment and as a backup winter larder for wildlife. Not all will be gobbled by birds: they aren't keen on skimmias or *Gaultheria procumbens*, and hollies often remain fully laden well into the new year.

1 Even a lone berrying plant, brought to the fore in a pot, can enliven a space. *Vaccinium vitis-idaea* 'Fireballs' (lingonberry or cowberry) is a robust ericaceous (use acidic compost!) evergreen that flowers and fruits freely, even in shade. Produced on compact self-fertile plants, the edible red

berries are usually plucked fairly early by birds, but watching them gorge is a treat in itself.

2 Arranged at uneven heights and spaced to flaunt their individual merits, edible blueberries, chilli peppers and cucamelon (*Melothria scabra*) are set with pure ornamentals, creating a fully rounded seasonal scene. *Hypericum* 'Miracle Night' contributes near-black (poisonous) berries and dark foliage that helps both the pink gentian and heather gleam, while terracotta lends a warmth to the picture.

3 Large and decorative harvested fruits, such as gourds and squashes, can be used to inject a display of pots with extra colour and interest. For impact, concentrate them in a group rather than dotting them about: arranged in a wooden crate or a large bowl, they'll achieve an eye-drawing focal point.

4 Despite their common name of 'barberry', the majority of berberis are grown for their colourful foliage or flowers rather than their berries, yet I think they are highly decorative, if not exactly showy. They vary considerably in shape and colour. Those of Japanese barberry (*B. thunbergii*), here, are bright red and hang on long after the leaves have shed.

5 *Hypericum* x *inodorum* 'Magical Pumpkin' is one of many recently introduced cultivars boasting conspicuous fruits in relatively subtle shades, and with the bonus of rich yellow summer flowers.

6 Although their fruits are not the longest lasting, few plants are quite as brilliant in berry as the firethorns or pyracantha (here 'Orange Glow'). Vigorous growing, they form large, thorny and long-lived shrubs but are useful in bigger containers in the shorter term. They can also be pruned and neatly trained to prolong their potted life.

THE TURN OF LEAVES

For most, the mere mention of autumn conjures uplifting images of deciduous trees dressed in brilliant shades. This fiery annual spectacle, which is the result of chlorophyll draining from old leaves preparing to fall, is surely the highlight of the season. Such splendour is not confined to large gardens, parkland and the natural landscape: there are many container-worthy small trees, shrubs and a few perennials that colour up reliably as autumn wears on. Some turn colour over many weeks, while others are more rapid in their change and shed quickly. Healthy plants in sheltered confines will put on the longest show.

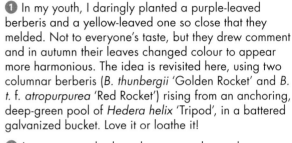

1 In my youth, I daringly planted a purple-leaved berberis and a yellow-leaved one so close that they melded. Not to everyone's taste, but they drew comment and in autumn their leaves changed colour to appear more harmonious. The idea is revisited here, using two columnar berberis (*B. thunbergii* 'Golden Rocket' and *B. t. f. atropurpurea* 'Red Rocket') rising from an anchoring, deep-green pool of *Hedera helix* 'Tripod', in a battered galvanized bucket. Love it or loathe it!

2 Japanese maples have become such popular container plants as to be held in contempt by some. Admittedly, I now have fewer than I once did, but when a plant offers so much you have to take advantage. All

excel in containers, although
the more compact cultivars
are worth seeking out, and the
cut-leaf 'dissectum' types with
their domed, gently weeping
habit top my list. Bright green
turned gold and amber, *Acer
palmatum* Dissectum Viride
Group is the centrepiece here:
its mounded form and warm
tones are echoed and expanded
by accompanying pots of
Heucherella 'Brass Lantern', *H.*
'Art Deco' and, in a rust-adorned
soup tin, carpeting *Acaena
microphylla* 'Kupferteppich'.
Equally, the greens of the
tall grasses behind and the
foreground fern help accentuate
the vibrancy of the maple.

③ Many smaller trees can be
enjoyed in containers for part
of their life, but they must be
decorative for several months at
least to warrant the effort. Many
aren't, but liquidambars (sweet
gum) absolutely are. They are
the go-to trees for long-lasting
autumn interest: expect multiple
colours on the same tree, cycling
through glowing shades as they
ready to drop. When their leaves
have long been swept up, their
well-branched, pyramidal shape
makes sweet gums ideal for
stringing with Christmas lights.
I grow my trees in large plastic
containers (with handles) that
make the trees more moveable
(and relatively easy to repot or
root-prune), then disguise the
plastic with timber, sections of
railway sleeper, sackcloth or,
as here, roof tiles and other
planted containers.

THE GLOWING SEASON

Even those who prefer sophisticated cool tones are certain to be seduced by the intensely vibrant shades of autumn. Colours from the warmer end of the spectrum appear to glow even more brightly in the ever-mellowing autumnal light, and their appeal is heightened. There's no shortage of striking foliage, from a range of evergreen and deciduous plants, as well as fruits and late flowers, that can readily be gathered in containers sited in key positions to maintain a colourful focus for autumn's duration.

❶ This vivid offering of trailing *Sedum* 'Lemon Ball', *Heuchera* 'Ginger Ale' and sword-leaved *Libertia* 'Taupo Blaze' will last until the first heavy frost damages the attention-grabbing ornamental chilli peppers (*Capsicum annuum* 'Medusa'). If the weather becomes a threat, shift the container to a cool porch or conservatory where it can be enjoyed throughout the season.

❷ Bold and simple, so guaranteed to catch the eye, this pairing of minty-green *Carex comans* 'Frosted Curls' and daisy-flowered *Rudbeckia* Summerina 'Orange' spans midsummer through autumn. While the spent rudbeckia blooms are highly attractive, I remove them in order to keep the flowers coming; it is only late in the season that I leave some petal-stripped cones for winter structure.

③ Summer survivors join autumn newbies to create a shamelessly vibrant bank of flowers, fruit and foliage, the rich colours intensified under moody skies. Purple-leaved *Perilla frutescens* var. *crispa* is starting to fail after a full summer of service, but *Pelargonium* 'Vancouver Centennial' and *Solenostemon scutellarioides* 'Campfire' (coleus) are still going strong. Trios of dwarf chrysanthemums and of chilli peppers are coming to their zenith, while contrast of form comes from the strap-like leaves of *Phormium* 'Chocomint' and, in the background, a soft mound of *Stipa tenuissima*.

④ Useful container plants for full sun or light shade, violas are available in a mesmerizing range of colours and regular dead-heading will persuade them to flower for months. Lettuce 'Red Oak Leaf' and round carrots offer a fitting and calming foil to these busy but cheery blooms.

⑤ A diminutive plant with impact, *Nertera depressa* (coral bead plant) is most often grown indoors but will brighten a sheltered spot outdoors until the frosts descend. Rusted metal, weathered timber and aged terracotta help the colour pop.

SEED HEADS & SENESCENCE

As the season winds on, many annuals and perennials fade gracefully, slowly withering to leave structural stems and intricate seed cases. Their decaying presence is even more joyous when strung with dew-laden cobwebs or iced in hoar frost, as winter creeps in. Over time, some will change pose or collapse completely, while others stand proud until cut down manually in spring. In the not-so-distant past, gardeners were positively encouraged to be autumnally neat but, thankfully, things have moved on and we now savour senescence, considering carefully before chopping down or snipping off.

① Often, a container may be hidden by its contents without detriment. In certain instances, though, a pot is of such beauty that it must be honoured. Ground-covering perennial *Persicaria affinis* 'Darjeeling Red' is trimmed regularly so as not to compromise the architectural lines of the reinforced concrete planter and, in its straw-like state, fountain-shaped *Molinia caerulea* subsp. *caerulea* 'Heidebraut' (purple moor-grass) tones amiably.

2 In a garden, decay can be beguiling. I almost prefer *Agapanthus* 'Charlotte' in its orange-yellow and biscuity autumn garb than the green and blue of summer. The arched-over, dying leaves are echoed in front by the long, curved fruits of the ornamental chilli pepper and trailing *Sedum* 'Lemon Ball'. Later, the leaves will turn mushy, so a little judicious tidying becomes necessary. Although more stems may topple, the majority of the skeletal seed heads will persist until spring.

3 When the light catches them, the feathery plumes of many taller grasses, such as well-named *Miscanthus sinensis* 'Morning Light', appear electrified and twinkle like a thousand tiny LEDs.

4 *Pennisetum alopecuroides* 'Red Head' is an excellent mid-height grass for containers. Ideally, position it where its fountain-like form is emphasized.

5 *Persicaria* 'Darjeeling Red' displays its browned and gently withered leaves alongside those in peak condition to give a two-tone appearance.

6 Through spring and summer *Athyrium niponicum* var. *pictum* (painted lady fern) requires a veil of shade to prevent its delicate leaves turning crisp and brown. As they wither it no longer matters, and out it comes to a spot where the effect of sunlight through its leaves can be marvelled at.

7 The often brightly coloured stems of grasses are an effective foil to the more muted stalks and seed heads of perennials, including agapanthus.

8 It's fascinating to note the change in plants from one end of the season to the other. This purple moor-grass became increasingly splayed but, even at the point of full collapse, it maintained an appeal.

9 As autumn progresses, the rugged, ribbed leaves of hostas turn buttery yellow, then russet edged, before becoming steadily bleached of all colour.

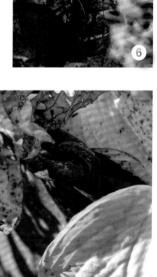

WINTER

EARLY WINTER

Come early winter, even the most brilliantly planted gardens are reduced to a stark frame. Plants in containers are at their most welcome now and even one or two small but well-planted pots can lift the spirits. They will more often be viewed through a window or in passing, so position them accordingly.

Handsome-leaved evergreens are the heroes of winter containers, their often colourful leaves stepping up to help overcome a seasonal lack of flowers. Involve coloured stems, buds-in-waiting, glossy berries and structural seed heads and there's plenty to work with. It's a fine discipline to be less reliant on flowers, whatever the time of year.

❶ Ornamental kales and cabbages, bred for leaf colour and form rather than taste, are useful autumn and early winter fillers. They sit more comfortably with fellow foliage plants than with flowers. As the season draws on they can look tatty but ensuring they are neither too wet nor too dry for prolonged periods (and protecting them from snails) will lengthen their aesthetic life. Keeping them in individual pots and 'plunging' them among their companions rather than planting out aids watering and makes for easy replacement, if necessary.

2 A tapestry of textures and restrained shades, this simple gathering of evergreen variegated lemon thyme (*Thymus citriodorus* 'Variegatus'), white winter-flowering heath (*Erica* x *darleyensis* f. *albiflora* 'Silberschmelze') and green-leaved ivies (*Hedera helix* 'Tripod') reliably maintains its composure throughout the darker months. Prairie grass (*Stipa tenuissima*) provides a tactile backdrop that sways mesmerizingly in the breeze and filters the pallid winter sun. The lichen-encrusted trough is well matched to its contents. Some garden centres discount old stock that has already begun to weather, although others may ask a premium.

3 A frosty coating sparkles on dinky evergreen *Thymus citriodorus* 'Variegatus'.

4 An easy-to-achieve 'pots in a pot' set up maximizes space and flexibility. Camellias would not tolerate this as permanent underplanting but, for the span of a single winter, no harm is done. This 'lollipop'- trained specimen lives in a large plastic pot sunk far enough down inside the purposely tall, ornamental terracotta container to allow its associates room to rest comfortably above. Separately wrapping the root ball of each plant in hessian or fine mesh makes them easier to squeeze in than if in rigid pots. Packed in tightly, they shelter and insulate each other.

5 Ornamental cabbage, *Ophiopogon planiscapus* 'Nigrescens' (black mondo) and *Corokia cotoneaster* huddle beneath *Camellia sasanqua*.

6 My early adoration of rhododendrons has never extended to camellias – except for the underappreciated autumn- and early winter-flowering *C. sasanqua* and its cultivars. They are neat, bushy and perfumed.

PREVIOUS PAGES Pots of late winter-flowering bulbs in shades of blue, including *Iris reticulata* 'Katharine Hodgkin', *I.r.* 'Harmony' and *I.r.* 'Clairette', are huddled in a sheltered corner near the house, Here they can be enjoyed without even having to venture out.

FESTIVE POTS

Christmas is a time when evergreens – from sprigs to entire trees – are traditionally lopped for indoor decoration, but many growing plants also deliver festive cheer, indoors and out. Numerous red-berried shrubs offer instant festivity, as do symbolic evergreens – most notably, of course, the holly (ilex) and the ivy (hedera): there are container-worthy varieties of each. Tough evergreen conifers, in particular pines, spruces and silver firs, lend themselves to adornment with bows and sparkly micro lights, all enhanced by the warmth of terracotta. There is no reason not to blend live plants with cut: I have a potted hazel (*Corylus avellana* 'Contorta') that, each December, becomes a 'mistletoe tree'. Most who spot it double-take and smile at the convincing execution.

① Coloured stems, evergreens and berries combine to achieve an imposing festive gesture that continues its appeal well into the new year. *Cornus alba* 'Sibirica' (dogwood) forms a sizeable shrub but can be kept in a large pot for a few years, especially if pruned hard each spring: this forces new stems of the brightest colour. Encircling, evergreen perennial *Euphorbia characias* 'Silver Swan' is clad in bright, cream-margined foliage, tamed by a dense green pool of prostrate-growing *Juniperus procumbens* 'Nana'. Less attractive to birds than most, the glowing red berries of *Skimmia japonica* 'Red Diamonds' hang around for months.

② While in bloom, *Helleborus niger* 'Christmas Carol' deserves attention. Lift it up and give it agreeable companions (*see* ⑦).

③ Ordinarily, I'd shy away from overuse of plants with variegated leaves and I almost never mix them, but at Christmas those rules dissolve. Here butter-yellow-margined *Euonymus fortunei* 'Emerald 'n' Gold' clashes gloriously with pink-red *Coprosma* 'Fire Burst'.

④ Stalwart winter heath, *Erica* x *darleyensis* f. *albiflora* 'Silberschmelze', has an iron constitution that contributes handily to the December garden.

⑤ *Skimmia japonica* 'Red Diamonds' and *Juniperus procumbens* 'Nana' benefit seasonally from their garnish of frost.

⑥ A wooden seed tray offers a stable station for a huddle of small terracotta pots, enabling a flexible display you can expand, rearrange and even enjoy indoors over Christmas. Come New Year, swap the cyclamens for a succession of flowering bulbs, such as irises and dwarf narcissi. Retaining its large red berries well into spring, evergreen *Gaultheria procumbens* (checkerberry) lives for years. The unplanted pots add texture, warmth and contrast but also prevent the planted ones toppling.

⑦ Raised on a table or chair and provided a complementary backdrop, even the most modest-sized plantings can impact the stripped winter landscape. Here *Helleborus niger* 'Christmas Carol', white-flowered winter heath, trailing ivy and *Gaultheria procumbens* comfortably colonize a decaying but characterful wooden box.

MIDWINTER

In the depths of winter, it is only the most committed who garden to any extent and just the bravest plants that bloom, but there's still much that thrills. While my own winter containers are mostly huddled near the house, I purposely position one or two (frostproof) pots of hardier plants, such as winter heaths, skimmias and hellebores, where they are likely to receive a spangle of hoar frost or light snow. The majority of seasonal plants offered by garden centres and nurseries just after Christmas will have been grown under glass, though, so shelter any you buy as much as possible – especially if the weather closes in.

❶ Though battered, this shallow copper bucket is a constant favourite. It suits many plants and sites and can even be suspended as an acceptable version of a hanging basket. Age has bestowed it much character and I happily recall the numerous plants it has housed throughout its long, repurposed life. Here, free-flowering *Cyclamen coum* floats with *Helleborus* x *ballardiae* HGC 'Merlin' above a weave of *Trifolium repens* 'Atropurpureum'. The handful of snowdrops (*Galanthus elwesii*) nods animatedly but neither they nor the cyclamens are happy in containers long term, so rehome them later beneath deciduous shrubs where they will multiply.

2 *Helleborus* HGC 'Pink Frost' blooms at full pelt for at least a couple of months, with a final flourish in early spring. As with all hellebores, the ageing blooms continue the appeal.

3 and **4** Witch hazels are a true winter highlight. Although they naturally form large, spreading shrubs, if carefully pruned after flowering, they should thrive in large pots of acidic compost for many years. Delicately perfumed *Hamamelis* x *intermedia* 'Arnold Promise' is among the most reliably floriferous. It is accompanied here by lime-green and double yellow hellebores (Lenten rose hybrids), irises 'Clairette' and 'Katharine Hodgkin' and a skirt of variegated sedges (*Carex oshimensis* 'Everlime' and *C. o.* 'Eversheen'). This is strictly a flight of fancy, in that the plants are packed in for effect and will succeed together only for a single winter. Nevertheless, the spectacle is worth the effort.

5 The vintage wooden trough here hosts a simple, inexpensive, textural assembly of aromatic *Thymus vulgaris* (common thyme), pink-flowered *Erica* x *darleyensis* 'Darley Dale' (winter heath), *Libertia ixioides* 'Taupo Blaze', *Ophiopogon planiscapus minimus* and squiggly *Juncus effusus* f. *spiralis* (corkscrew rush). Echoing the fan-shaped libertia, pinkish-red *Phormium* 'Jester' sits behind in a separate pot.

DWARF IRIS TIME

Opportunity to bring diminutive, early flowering plants near is welcome during months when the weather can be miserable. None are more deserving of scrutiny than reticulate irises, which bloom in tune with snowdrops and crocuses. I'm ever more smitten with them. They have been gaining in popularity and the range of cultivars is widening. They are at their most potent potted into complementary containers and presented up close. Although their blooming is a sure sign that spring draws near, they are resolute winter flowerers and far more robust than they appear. They are an absolute 'must grow'.

❶ Dark blue *Iris* 'Clairette' and pale *I.* 'Katharine Hodgkin' are mutually flattering. Pots of different depth show the flowers off in tiers, rather than less effectively all at the same height.

❷ Decoratively patterned pots add colour and interest but make sure they accentuate rather than overshadow their contents. This Delft-style pot neatly complements slender *Iris* 'Painted Lady'.

❸ A hollow brick is as an ideal platform for dwarf irises (here *I. histrioides* 'Lady Beatrix Stanley'). The pockets perfectly space the bulbs, allowing the blooms to be appreciated for their architectural shapeliness as well as their intricate detail – a joy missed when they are crowded together en masse. This is also an artful way to present new cultivars that can cost as much per bulb as for ten of older varieties. In autumn, push fine mesh into the bottom of each hollow, pop in a single bulb, then fill with gritty compost. Top off with a layer of grit to protect the petals from splashes.

❹ Potted individually, dwarf irises (here 'Katherine's Gold') can be displayed with a degree of separation and a touch of variety in order to appreciate their beauty.

❺ Irises 'Katharine Hodgkin' and 'Katherine's Gold' sing out against a rich-green mat of tiny-leaved evergreen *Euonymus fortunei* 'Kewensis'. Carpeting thymes and saxifrages are alternatives.

LATE WINTER

Calendars aside, as with all the seasonal handovers, the line between winter and spring is blurred. The last days of the darker months are happily marked by a steadily widening array of blooms: hellebores are still the stand-out stars but dwarf irises and cyclamens begin stepping aside for miniature daffodils, primroses and crocuses, among many. Then comes that indefinable but palpable moment when the air and the light speak more of spring than of winter. This is among the most exciting times of year and the point when the advance investment of potting as many bulbs as you dared the previous October and November begins, thrillingly, to pay off.

1 Sections of wooden pallets and railway sleepers are stacked to create tiers that exhibit a variety of plants and pots. Each is clearly visible in its own right, while also endorsing the whole. Towards the front are *Hebe* 'Blue Star', *Skimmia japonica* 'Moerings 1', hellebores, cyclamen and iris, with *Helleborus* HGC 'Pink Frost', *Viburnum tinus* 'Eve Price', and irises 'Pauline' and 'Katharine Hodgkin', raised behind. A now-bolting, but no less attractive, ornamental cabbage from earlier in the season helps anchor the colour scheme.

2 I've enjoyed this same *Euonymus fortunei* 'Kewensis' for nearly thirty years. A resilient, mat-forming evergreen, it is supremely adaptable and looks comfortably at home in any style of pot. It's a pool of calm and an impeccable foil to a host of other plants from dwarf narcissi to ferns, as well as the irises on page 109.

3 Saucer-flowered *Helleborus* (Rodney Davey Marbled Group) 'Molly's White', wispy *Carex* 'Milk Chocolate' and ebony-leaved *Ophiopogon planiscapus* 'Nigrescens' encircle *Phormium* 'Bronze Baby' to supply a long-lasting, architecturally pleasing visual effect. The capacious, pale glazed pot tones perfectly with the hellebores, so contributes quietly but crucially.

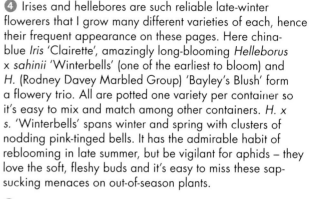

4 Irises and hellebores are such reliable late-winter flowerers that I grow many different varieties of each, hence their frequent appearance on these pages. Here china-blue *Iris* 'Clairette', amazingly long-blooming *Helleborus x sahinii* 'Winterbells' (one of the earliest to bloom) and *H.* (Rodney Davey Marbled Group) 'Bayley's Blush' form a flowery trio. All are potted one variety per container so it's easy to mix and match among other containers. *H. x s.* 'Winterbells' spans winter and spring with clusters of nodding pink-tinged bells. It has the admirable habit of reblooming in late summer, but be vigilant for aphids – they love the soft, fleshy buds and it's easy to miss these sap-sucking menaces on out-of-season plants.

5 Even a modest injection of colour, such as a single hyacinth, can lift an otherwise static display. *Hyacinthus* 'Pink Pearl' brings a focal jolt of instant, if temporary, colour (and fragrance) to a long-serving gathering of evergreens, including *Viburnum tinus* 'Eve Price', *Nandina domestica* 'Seika' (syn. 'Obsessed'), *Helleborus* HGC 'Pink Frost' and *Skimmia japonica* 'Rubella', on which the red buds are just beginning to burst.

⑥ Where there's room, placing some pots to allow them breathing space and you to squeeze or sit among them is an inviting format. Varying their height so the shape and detail of each container is visible gives them greater individual sway and makes for a lively scene. Spacing also allows for easier maintenance and scrutiny. Adding accessories, such as slabs of slate or pebbles, makes more of a space using fewer plants and pots – especially useful in winter. I'd intended to use pale yellow hyacinths but the pinks had more flower and, although not quite the right shade, still delivered an eye-catching pop of central colour. *Heuchera* 'Blackberry Jam', *Viburnum tinus* 'Eve Price', *Nandina domestica* 'Seika' (syn. 'Obsessed'), phormium, hellebores and *Skimmia japonica* 'Rubella' formed a surrounding frame.

⑦ & ⑧ This is the same pot of *Phormium* 'Maori Queen' and *Helleborus* 'Angel Glow' as in ⑥, photographed again the following winter. With minimal effort on my part, they thrived together for a couple of years before becoming overcrowded. Many hybrid hellebores resent too much pot space and hate overwatering, so I reckon the fleshy-rooted phormium helped drain away excess water. A light dusting of snow is a delightful adornment but heavier falls are best shaken off, if possible.

⑨ Having fallen from favour decades ago, conifers are making a comeback. Interesting new introductions and innovative methods of training are helping reinvent them. Slow-growing and compact cultivars are dependable container plants, whether used as specimens or grouped, although some are far more charismatic than others, so research is advisable. Bun-shaped *Thuja occidentalis* 'Golden Tuffet' and ground-covering *Juniperus communis* 'Green Carpet' are both worth seeking out. Especially handsome and characterful are pines such as *Pinus mugo* 'Ophir', the golden vertical centrepiece of this mini-scape.

⑩ Snow lodges decoratively on the whorled branches of pines – I grow several dwarf varieties specifically for this delight!

PICKING PLANTS & CHOOSING POTS

WHAT TO GROW

PREVIOUS PAGE
Grown from bulbs planted in late summer or early autumn, *Scilla peruviana* is a showy Mediterranean native that is more reliable in pots where it is easier to provide sharp drainage than in the open ground.

LEFT Even mighty oaks can be grown in pots for a number of years and it is a pleasure to watch them grow and develop. Eventually they will need more root room so, if possible, have somewhere lined up.

Almost any plant will grow in a pot. Not all will thank you for it, and some won't sufficiently reward the effort but, excitingly, the range of plants that excel in containers is extensive and diverse. Many more container-worthy varieties are introduced each year and so choosing can be simultaneously thrilling and daunting. Take your time, though, and relish every moment. A number of the most attractive and useful plants that I've come to rely on are gathered in this book. These next pages offer the briefest introduction. A wander on the internet will provide more detail.

Plants for containers can be roughly divided into two major categories: long-term structural specimens that will serve for many years, and temporary seasonal subjects that may only be in flower for weeks or months. The latter comprises annuals, biennials, tender perennials, bulbs and vegetables, while trees, shrubs, conifers, climbing plants, perennials and grasses are among the more permanent.

In order to earn a place in one of my containers, a plant must fulfil certain basic requirements. Primarily, it should have as long a period of interest as possible. There are exceptions, including tulips and lilies, but nobody wishes to replant every few weeks. The more seasons in which a plant has something to offer the better, especially where space is at a premium. Plants that flower, fruit and are dressed in attractive leaves head the list. A first-rate long-term container plant should also ideally be relatively compact and not over-vigorous, although this is a loose rule that can be broken, especially for dramatic effect.

Another consideration is the specific cultural requirement of each plant. This is especially important for longer-term subjects. A little homework will help ensure that plant and site are well matched and that you are able to cater for its needs as closely as possible. Because you can exercise a degree of control over their growing conditions, certain plants may even perform better than if in the ground.

There's no point, for instance, in planting sun-loving marguerite daisies (argyranthemum) in a container plunged into half light under a tree, as their growth will be straggly and their flowers sparse. Similarly, Japanese maples that thrive in cool, sheltered spots are not sensible candidates for a sun trap or an exposed, windy position. I've made plenty of mistakes myself but in so doing have learnt that you never know what you may get away with. The saving grace with containers is that if you recognize an error in good time, you can relocate your wrongly sited plant to a more appropriate spot swiftly and with relative ease.

Trees & shrubs

1 *Acer palmatum* 'Orange Dream' (Japanese maple)

2 *Leptospermum scoparium* 'Red Ensign'

3 *Daphne bholua* 'Jacqueline Postill'

4 *Pieris japonica* 'Little Heath'

5 *Dicksonia antarctica* (tree fern)

6 *Hydrangea macrophylla* 'Blackberry Pie'

7 *Rhododendron* 'Percy Wiseman'

Trees and shrubs provide ever-present structure vital to long-term container displays. By employing a variety of woody plants, a multilayered, continually changing, year-round potted oasis is readily attainable. If you invest in a few really hard-working framework plants other more temporary additions will be all the more effective.

The ancient art of bonsai is illustration enough that even majestic trees, such as oaks and pines, can be contained, albeit in a very labour-intensive way. Many trees can be encouraged to live in containers of sufficient size for a surprising number of years without quite such effort and there are several that I've seen thriving for a decade or more. Among them are *Cercis canadensis*, *Fagus sylvatica* 'Purpurea Pendula', *Liquidambar styraciflua*, *Amelanchier lamarckii*, *Salix erythroflexuosa* and *Rhus typhina* 'Laciniata'. The latter two can be cut down hard each spring, as can *Eucalyptus gunnii*, so are quite manageable. For gardens where there is no other height, shrubs such as holly, photinia and privet, top-worked as half-standards or clipped as topiary columns or lollipops, are a consideration.

Evergreens are natural long-term choices for containers, especially those that are compact or slow-growing. They are reliable mainstays and work hard as a foil to more colourful plants with relatively fleeting offerings. Their longevity makes them worth the initial investment. There are many to choose between, including those with brightly variegated foliage and others with handsome, architectural leaves. Phormiums (New Zealand flax) are strictly evergreen clump-forming perennials but have a permanence that affords them a mention here as excellent for sun or shade. Unlike woody shrubs, they may be tipped out and split once they become too large, so are easily rejuvenated. Other favourites include *Fatsia polycarpa*, choisya, pieris, mahonia and *Corokia* x *virgata* 'Sunsplash' (I've had one in the same pot for fifteen years). In recent years, as new cultivars have appeared, I've become increasingly enamoured of coprosmas from New Zealand. Although requiring protection in colder locales, their compact habit and bright leaves render them very desirable. Pittosporum is another New Zealander with newer, neater cultivars that lend themselves to container use.

Dwarf and slow-growing conifers are invaluable, especially in winter, and deserve greater popularity. Far from being unchanging, many cycle through different hues with the seasons, becoming burnished in winter and turning brighter as the fresh new foliage breaks in spring. Pines in particular are full of character and the slower-growing kinds will live on in a pot for years. Prostrate junipers are tough as old boots and team attractively with other densely structured plants such as winter-flowering heaths.

Deciduous shrubs that are a short time in flower such as deutzia, syringa or even magnolias don't really earn their keep, but others with foliage interest including physocarpus, acers (Japanese maples) and sorbaria are a different matter.

Hardy perennials

Perennials – non-woody plants that live for at least two years (though often, indefinitely) – are grouped into those that are winter hardy and so can be left outdoors year round, and tender types (see *Annuals, biennials and tender perennials,* page 126) that must be protected from cold. Both groups include numerous first-class container dependables.

One of the loveliest qualities of many hardy perennials suited to pots is that they will change appearance and pace as the seasons progress. In March, hostas are represented by plump pointed buds which then unfold and expand ever more rapidly as the days lengthen. By early May, these supreme container plants are at their most handsome and the sculpted leaves are later joined by silver-mauve or white blooms. In autumn, the leaves wither and bleach very appealingly. In the case of pulmonarias or lungworts the welcome flowers appear first with the often spotted or silvered leaves enlarging as the blooms fade. Woodland plants such as epimediums, brunnera and ferns will happily oblige in pots in a shady corner. The choice of ferns is wondrous and displaying them in pots allows full appreciation of their sculptural forms. Painted lady fern (*Athyrium niponicum* var. *pictum*), Copper shield fern (*Dryopteris erythrosora*) and the very fine *Athyrium filix-femina* 'Frizelliae' are three I would never give up. As with most perennials, if they begin to look tired or untidy, a bit of a chop will rejuvenate them.

Many hardy perennials are excellent for pollinators and have an informal naturalistic air that is a sought-after quality. The most container-worthy are those that either flower over a long period or display good-looking leaves. *Verbena officinalis* var. *grandiflora* 'Bampton', sanguisorba, gaura, *Allium hookeri* 'Zorami' all fit, as do shorter, less vigorous persicarias including *P. amplexicaulis* 'Pink Elephant', *P. a.* 'Blackfield' and *P. microcephala* 'Red Dragon'. Many grasses and sedges also pander to the trend for more relaxed planting, contributing softness and texture, although I use them more sparingly than I once did. I usually opt for more flowing species such as hakonechloa, eragrostis and *Stipa barbata*, along with particularly wispy and transparent panicums and molinias. *Pennisetum* 'Fairy Tails' and *Miscanthus* 'Red Cloud', also each deserve a mention.

As grasses prove, leaves are equally as important visually as flowers. Arguably more so, and it's a real plus if foliage plants are evergreen or, at some point during the season, they also produce conspicuous blooms. A well thought out display relies on these plants to provide body, middle ground and a tempering foil to showy blooms. Among the best are heucheras, tiarellas and heucherellas (a hybrid of the first two). Thanks to their highly attractive leaves, neat habit and frothy sprays of delicate blooms, all are superb for containers in any season. Many euphorbias or spurges also fall into this category and provide height in the centre or at the back of the pot.

Whilst some perennials work best mixed with other plants in the same pot, the likes of agapanthus, hostas, heucheras and melianthus make an impact even when unaccompanied.

1 *Brunnera macrophylla* 'Jack Frost'

2 *Dryopteris erythrosora*

3 *Heuchera* 'Marmalade' and *Trifolium repens* 'Atropurpureum'

4 *Echinacea purpurea* 'White Swan'

5 *Rudbeckia* 'Summerina Orange' (Summerina Series)

6 *Festuca glauca* 'Intense Blue'

Flowering bulbs

1. *Iris 'Katharine Hodgkin'*

2. *Scilla siberica*

3. *Scilla peruviana*

4. *Erythronium 'Pagoda'*
(dog's tooth violet)

5. *Anemone blanda*
'white splendour'

6. *Narcissus 'Rip van Winkle'*

7. *Tulipa 'Weber's Parrot'* with
Brunnera macrophylla 'Jack Frost'

8. *Hyacinthus 'Pink Pearl'*

PLANTING IN LAYERS

A reliable means of achieving a succession of colour in a single pot is to plant bulbs in layers, particularly if you are pushed for space. The optimum is three but in smaller pots two layers are more sensible and four in especially large pots. Plant the largest, latest-flowering bulbs at the bottom – they can be as deep as 30cm (12in) – and the earliest, smallest ones in the uppermost layer. Planted in a single layer, bulbs can be almost touching but multi-layers require wider spacing to allow the lower ones room to grow through. Ensure good drainage by mixing grit into the compost and, if possible, stand the pots on bricks or pot feet. Cover lower and intermediate layers with 5cm (2in) of compost and put the upper layer 10cm (4in) deep.

Were it not for the great variety of easy-to-grow flowering bulbs, corms and tubers, container gardeners would find colouring in the spring months considerably more challenging. The majority thrive in pots and, planted to flower in succession, they will span the entire season: from dwarf irises (see page 108) and pollen-laden crocuses that bloom on the winter–spring cusp to flamboyant tulips (see pages 40–45) that pave the way for summer.

Many types of bulb I grow only in pots, where they will not be accidentally disturbed when dormant and, as none are in flower for more than a few weeks, can be easily moved once faded. Some are potted into plastic pots and sat snugly inside ornamental containers whilst a few are plunged into deliberately left gaps among other seasonal plants and evergreens within larger pots. Inserting an empty pot of matching size when planting up provides space for them without disruption.

Others go directly into ornamental pots – usually just one or two varieties in each – to group together as they come into flower and easily shift when they are done. I also plant tulips and narcissi among leafy herbaceous perennials such as hostas, brunnera and persicaria so that when the latter come into growth they take over and hide the dying bulb foliage.

Most spring-flowering bulbs that excel in containers require an open, sunny position, although *Ornithogalum nutans*, erythroniums and trilliums are among the shade lovers. I'm especially fond of trilliums and although they aren't at their happiest when contained, they are easier to protect from snails which always decimate those I dare to plant out. Wind-resistant dwarf daffodils and narcissi can also handle a little shade and are a more canny bet than their taller cousins. Multi-headed ones, such as the Triandrus types which include my favourite 'Hawera', are especially good value. Many bear multiple stems, giving a more impactful display from fewer bulbs.

In pots, bulbs may be planted both deeper and more shallowly, as well as more closely, than if in the ground. This allows you to pack them in for an impressive display, although you should keep in mind the size and shape of their blooms: dwarf irises, for instance, are less effective in flower if they are too crowded. By staggering planting times then keeping most pots in a very cool place outdoors (most bulbs will tolerate very low temperatures) but bringing some under cover, you can anticipate a long continuation of colour.

Bulb catalogues ooze tempting varieties, and as well as repeating old favourites it's always great to discover new ones. Always check bulb size, particularly if buying mail order. The largest bulbs produce the most stems and largest, finest blooms so the price usually correlates to bulb size.

It's not just in spring that bulbs step up: summer- and autumn-flowering species, including alliums, dahlias, gladiolus, crocus, colchicums and nerines, are also invaluable. As long as you plant them at the right time – and in many instances that can be stretched – you can't go far wrong.

Tiny plants

1. *Pratia pedunculata* 'County Park'

2. *Rhodohypoxis baurii*

3. *Lithodora diffusa* 'Heavenly Blue'

4. *Saxifraga* Southside Seedling Group with thyme and sempervivum

5. *Lewisia cotyledon* hybrid

6. *Saxifraga* (Mossy Group) 'Peter Pan'

7. *Phlox subulata* 'Emerald Cushion Blue'

8. *Armeria pseudarmeria* 'Ballerina Red'

9. *Delosperma* 'Jewel of The Desert'

10. *Orostachys iwarenge* (Chinese hat or Chinese dunce cap)

11. *Trifolium repens* 'Dragon's Blood'

The tiniest of plants are generally more assured of a longer life in pots than in the garden soil, where they can all too soon become overshadowed. I refer mainly to gem-like alpine plants that enthusiasts and botanical gardens often afford dedicated glasshouses, but which the average gardener might find hard to site. I've lost so many diminutive specimens to envelopment by stronger growers and so I now limit myself to the few I keep in terracotta pots and troughs. Putting these plants in pots also means they can be viewed without getting on your hands and knees, and their individual needs can be catered for. Miniature worlds are enthralling for young and old alike, and growing tiny plants in pots helps teach us to appreciate intricate detail.

More readily available alpine species are not difficult to grow and so are great for beginner gardeners, and are long-lived if potted using very free-draining soil. However, many, such as fleshy-leaved lewisias, dainty alpine poppies (*Papaver alpinum*) and cushion saxifrages, will deteriorate if they get too wet, especially around the neckline, so add grit to the compost when potting and as a topdressing.

Densely carpeting plants such as fern-like leptinella, blue-flowered pratia, almost-microscopic raoulia, aromatic chamomile and creeping thymes (such as woolly-leaved *T. lanuginosus*) will quickly cover the surface of smaller pots. I tend to plant them in much-wider-than-high containers to accentuate their habit and achieve calming pools of leaves and bloom.

As a rule, tiny plants are best singled out in individual pots, although they can be very successful grouped together in one pot (or stone sink) provided they all like similar conditions and have compatible growth rates.

Provided acidic compost, a warm, sunny summer home and kept on the dry side through winter, dainty rhodohypoxis will form dense low clumps of narrow, hairy leaves studded in summer with starry blooms in many shades of pink. I can't think of a more spectacular tiny plant, except perhaps autumn-flowering gentians, which, again, need quite specific conditions in order to thrive. I've had considerably more success with them in pots of ericaceous compost than in specially prepared ground, but they still prove tricky to keep. The sheer beauty and intense colouring of their trumpet blooms, however, tempts me to keep trying. And next time you encounter a gentian flower, please look down its throat!

Finally, consider shrubby dwarf evergreens, like cushion hebes, deliciously scented *Daphne collina*, the most miniature and slow-growing conifers and flowering heaths and heathers with all their colouring leaves.

See *Raise them up*, page 31, and *Table tops*, page 78.

Annuals, biennials & tender perennials

The mainstay of many a summer container is half-hardy annuals and the ever-expanding group of tender or half-hardy perennials that are widely termed 'patio plants'. The range of both has exploded in the last few decades, and during my time as a container gardener. Once there seemed very little choice, whereas now it is quite the opposite. For the first mixed summer pot I planted, only fuchsias, geraniums (strictly zonal pelargoniums) and a few trailing foliage plants including *Helichrysum petiolare* were readily available to team with impatiens, petunias and lobelia. But then arrived the first trailing petunias and suddenly the floodgates opened. From South Africa came a whole host of jewel-like plants including diascias, osteospermums and nemesias that plant hybridizers worked on in earnest. Breeders continue to produce new and 'improved' varieties in ever more different colours and sizes to suit all tastes, though most, by their very nature, are not subtle!

Both daisy-flowered argyranthemums and osteospermums form floriferous bushy plants that are best potted as individual specimens and deadheaded for tidiness. The latter are offered in some astounding, almost luminous colours, bicolours and almost metallics that literally sparkle in sunlight. Petchoa – a cross between petunias and daintier trailing callibrachoas – is also available in tantalizing shades. Other must-haves are the curious scarlet-flowered *Cuphea* 'Torpedo', gentian-blue anagallis, trailing silver dichondra, leafy solenostemon (coleus), *Ipomoea batatas* and dainty cultivars of non-stop flowering *Euphorbia hypericifolia*.

When it comes to hardy annuals, I couldn't be without sunflowers for their larger-than-life cheerfulness and willingness to grow. There are plenty of dwarf kinds to choose from and I often underplant with petunias, calendulas and dwarf runner bean 'Hestia' for a riot. Sow them into paper or biodegradable fibre pots, or directly into their final homes. Most other easy hardy annuals such as cornflowers, calendulas, larkspur, nasturtiums, poppies and nigella are best sown directly, whether in blocks of each or as a random mix. They look great in wooden crates. Bear in mind, though, that these will not flower on through the entirety of summer in common with stalwart half-hardy annuals that include petunias, marigolds, lobelia, nicotiana, tagetes, cosmos, rudbeckia and *Begonia semperflorens*.

For spring, biennials such as wallflowers, bellis daisies and, of course, pansies and violas may be drafted in to complement hyacinths, narcissi and tulips, although I mostly accompany my bulbs with a less brightly coloured foil of leafy perennials. In autumn and winter, half-hardy mini cyclamens are invaluable. Although they'll suffer low temperatures, they are very susceptible to wet, so tuck them under open-sided cover.

1 *Osteospermum*

2 *Nemesia denticulata* 'Confetti'

3 *Pelargonium* 'Fireworks Red-white' (Fireworks Series)

4 *Cosmos* 'Xanthos'

5 *Centaurea cyanus* (cornflower)

6 *Gazania* 'Apache'

7 *Calibrachoa* 'Double Lemon' (Minifamous series)

BUYING PLANTS

When selecting seasonal plants, choose those that are compact, well branched and healthy looking over those that are spindly and yellowing. Choose specimens in bud rather than those in full flower and, if you dare, check the condition of the root system by carefully lifting the rootball out of the pot. Ideally, plants should be well rooted round the pot so the compost is held together but not such a thick mass that you can barely see any compost.

Annual climbing plants

1. *Ipomoea purpurea 'Grandpa Otts'* (Morning glory)

2. *Asarina scandens*

3. *Lathyrus odoratus 'Matucana'* (Sweet pea)

4. *Thunbergia alata 'Arizona Glow'*

5. *Rhodochiton atrosanguineum* (purple bell vine)

6. *Cobaea scandens*

7. *Tropaeolum peregrinum* (Canary creeper)

8. *Ipomoea lobata*

GROWING TIP

Most annual climbing plants are easy to grow from seed and once germinated will romp away quickly, climbing two metres (7 feet) or more by midsummer. Sow larger seeds in biodegradable pots, cardboard tubes or rolled up newspaper (I have a quirky little tool for making newspaper pots that my nieces and nephews enjoy using) as this avoids root disturbance when planting out and also cuts out the use of plastic.

Without this obliging group of plants, my own summer container displays would be seriously diminished and I've come to rely upon them. They are mostly of very easy culture and even just a few will make an impression. That said, there are several first-rate kinds that I grow in number every year, both in pots and in the ground as temporary screens. Scrambling up to two metres high or more in a season, they achieve considerable impact, greening and brightening areas that other annuals fail to reach. Many are as comfortable trailing as climbing and so are useful in multi-level displays, and all deliver vertical accent without hogging too much ground space so are especially welcome in smaller gardens.

Climbing via a variety of methods from tendrils to spiralling stems, all require some form of support, whether it is destined to be completely obscured or on-show as ornamental accompaniment. Mostly, I like at least a little of the frame visible as it will contrast with and complement the plant. Potential supports include other plants (they will romp up through large established shrubs and small trees), wires on walls, bamboo canes, trellis or crafted metal obelisks. Structures fashioned from pliable willow and free-standing wigwams of hazel stems or birch or lime branches are easy to erect, inexpensive and highly attractive in their own right. I also use salvaged scrap steel rods (especially those that are twisted and curved), copper tubing and concrete reinforcing mesh, which is more appealing once a layer of rust has formed and can be made into architectural features.

Strictly speaking, many that we term 'annual' climbing plants are actually tender perennials, such as highly floriferous thunbergias and elegant cobaea, that may be overwintered in a glasshouse or conservatory. Under the right conditions their growth rate is rapid and many make a midsummer spurt once their root system is fully established and filling the pot. In my experience, most flower better and more promptly (some like to keep you waiting a while before they bloom freely) if their roots are restricted. Relative to their ultimate size, I tend to plant in modest-sized pots of around 40cm/16in diameter, then feed weekly with a soluble fertilizer to sustain them through the latter half of summer and into autumn when many come into their own.

Among my can't-do-withouts are Canary creeper (*Tropaeolum peregrinum*), various morning glory (ipomoea), Spanish flag (*Ipomoea lobata*) and the incomparable purple bell vine (rhodochiton). The last is best trained around hoops or along horizontal wires to allow the curiously shaped 'bells' to dangle freely. Clambering up tall, strong hazel stems with runner beans in a capacious container, gourds are an annual talking point in my garden. Numerous other combinations spring to mind but the pairing of Spanish flag and black-eyed Susan (thunbergia) takes some beating. For other planting suggestions see *Quick climbers*, page 82.

Plants to eat

Even if growing for the crop isn't your priority, many edible plants are worth considering for looks alone. Many are equally as attractive as those grown purely for aesthetic reasons and as long as you avoid poisonous or irritant species, mixing productive plants with pure ornamentals is a successful way of enjoying both. Whatever your priority, growing cropping plants in pots allows easier control of their cultural conditions. As a rule, fruiting plants perform better without root competition and this is especially true of chilli peppers, sweet peppers, aubergines (eggplants) and tomatoes. I mostly pot them individually or in groups of the same variety then cluster them together, disguising plastic pots with hessian sacking and rope.

The majority of herbs, whether culinary or not, are deservedly popular plants for pots. Thymes, in all their variety, are supremely fit for purpose and I grow several different basils each year – they are very diverse in flavour and appearance. Well-grown plants of curled parsley resemble cloud topiary in miniature and so I plant them as early as possible to gain large specimens that won't miss a sprig or two every so often. Rosemary thrives in pots of free-draining compost and, as well as providing sprigs of aromatic foliage, flowers from early in the year.

Swiss chard offers colourful winter stalks for your pots as well as your plate; eat the young leaves as salad and cook older leaves like spinach. Another winter stalwart is curly kale. Runner beans and peas give height to a display (and pea shoots are delicious), although there are short-growing varieties of both that are ideal for growing in pots with dwarf French beans. Courgette plants are impressively architectural and, besides the fruits, the large showy flowers (or rather the buds) are also famously edible. Other plants with edible blooms include chives, pot marigold, borage, nasturtium and viola.

Carrots (round-headed are best, unless growing in deep containers), radishes, baby salad leaves and oriental greens are all ideally matched to wooden crates and trays; catering-sized food tins are perfect for tumbling tomatoes and chilli peppers. Naturally, most vegetables need a steady supply of water to produce a succession of quality produce but equally do not like to sit in water so make sure any repurposed containers drain freely.

Tree fruits grafted on to dwarfing rootstocks will also succeed in pots, and although you wouldn't expect massive crops the satisfying feeling that comes from growing even a handful of your own fruit makes any effort worthwhile. Although apple, plum and cherry are as attractive as any flowering tree, most fruit trees can look a little scruffy as the season progresses and so I ensure they are accompanied by a few annual climbing plants and other colourful plants to draw the eye. Acid-loving blueberries (*Vaccinium corymbosum*) are among the few bush fruits that thrive in containers and although self-fertile will produce greater crops if there are two varieties that bloom simultaneously to cross-pollinate.

1. *Borago officinalis* (borage)
2. *Melothria scabra* (cucamelon)
3. *Solanum lycopersicum* 'Tumbling Tom Red' (tomato)
4. *Vaccinium corymbosum* (blueberry)
5. *Cucurbita* (squash) in flower
6. *Phaseolus coccineus* 'Hestia' (dwarf runner bean)
7. *Solanum melongena* 'Baby Rosanna' (aubergine)
8. *Daucus carota* subsp. *sativus* 'Rondo' (carrot)
9. *Beta vulgaris* subsp *vulgaris* (chard or leaf beet)
10. *Capsicum annuum* 'Super Chilli' (edible/ornamental chilli pepper)

CHOOSING THE RIGHT POT

Any hollow object capable of holding growing medium that can drain freely is a potential plant pot. The possibilities of recycling and repurposing send the imagination wandering, while purpose-made containers are available in mind-blowing variety. Recent manufacturing advances have significantly and excitingly broadened the range of good-looking, durable and affordable options.

Looks are commonly the prime consideration when choosing pots, and all tastes are comprehensively catered for. Over time I've amassed an eclectic collection in every material, many pieces of which are cherished and irreplaceable. The majority are intentionally fairly plain, though enhanced with the patina that weathering and age bestow. Their definite shapes and unfussy designs enable them to sit comfortably together in many quite different settings. Size and proportion are also important buying criteria. On a broad expanse of paving, a cluster of small pots brings little impact, whereas one or more much larger ones can have real presence. Pocket-sized places need not be populated only with scaled-down pots: a large sculptural planter can dramatically hold sway in a modest courtyard.

Where space is at a premium, such as on a roof garden or balcony, square or rectangular pots that can be neatly abutted are a canny choice. Weight is also a consideration for roof gardens – and if you shift your pots around often. Give thought also to how much time you can commit to tending. Large containers will dry out less quickly, so it makes sense not to overdose on smaller ones unless you can attend to them most days, or they contain drought-tolerant plants. Always assess the ease of emptying a container for replanting: those that are narrower at their rim than at any point below present a serious challenge when removing pot-bound shrubs and so are better suited to short-term planting.

Sculptural containers formed of superior materials carry hefty price tags, but you can equally spend very little. Some of my most frequently used pots cost only the courage it took to rescue them, with permission, from skips. Quality made-for-the-job plant containers, though, are a shrewd investment that, barring mishap, will delight for a lifetime.

Pots are available in all shapes and sizes, and an ever-widening range of styles and materials. Shop around for those most suited to your taste and your garden.

Which pot?

TERRACOTTA

Universally approved by growers across many centuries, clay is the versatile, dug-from-the-ground material most widely used to make ornamental garden pots. The colour and finish vary, depending on where, how and from what type of clay they were made, and this variability is among the many charms of earthenware. Meaning 'baked earth' in Italian, brownish-red 'terracotta' is by far the most favoured and weather-resilient clay for outdoor use. Its warm tones complement absolutely any plant; I cannot think of an exception.

The majority of terracotta containers for sale in garden centres are cost-effectively formed in moulds but hand-thrown, artisan pots are also to be found. Although relatively expensive, these are real treasures and are talking points in themselves. Some of my own more unusual clay pots I've not seen for sale since I bought them and so I am highly protective of them. Due to the near-infinite variety of shapes, sizes and styles – from the romantically over-ornate to the practically plain – that can be fashioned from clay, there's surely a terracotta pot to suit every outdoor space. Consequently, terracotta containers are likely to be always the most popular for gardens and the most reliable and easy to incorporate visually. They are certainly the most constantly in use among my own pots and usually my first choice when selecting homes for precious new acquisitions. At least 60 per cent of the pots I own are clay.

Weather-licked, lichen-mottled terracotta oozes character and is beauteous in its own right. Earthenware ages at different rates, depending on its consistency, how it was fired and its finish: rougher-cast surfaces are usually more swiftly transformed. In my experience, the most effective way to speed the process is not to plaster your pots in yogurt but – whether planted or not – to fill them with compost and keep it moist. Even when not in use as homes for treasured plants, diminutive clay pots lend themselves to being artistically arranged in rows or stacks – or filled with other materials, such as pebbles or pine cones.

Terracotta is the most widely used material for ornamental plant pots and has been for centuries. All plants are enhanced when teamed with terracotta, without exception.

Among the practical pluses of terracotta is that its porosity allows plant roots sufficient oxygen to develop healthily and quickly, as well as helping to regulate the temperature so the root system is kept cool in summer and insulated during winter. On the negative side, the compost in porous pots dries out more rapidly than in those made of impervious materials. Counter this by lining the sides (but not the base) with used compost bags.

Personal taste heavily influences any purchase, but always buy the best-quality terracotta pots that you can afford, and check that they are guaranteed as frost resistant. In frost-prone areas cheap examples will seldom last their first winter outdoors, whereas well-made pieces fired at a high temperature should last indefinitely. I learnt the hard way the false economy of buying inexpensive pots that are easily damaged through weather or clumsiness.

GOOD LOOKS

In winter the aesthetic appeal of the container itself becomes even more relevant because it is less likely to be disguised by a profusion of growth, as in summer. Choose a particularly good-looking or interesting pot or pots and you are already halfway towards achieving an eye-catching display

Generally, I'd recommend using pots 40cm (16in) plus in diameter for winter displays. This is because the greater the volume of compost, the less likely it is to freeze right through. When the roots and compost freeze, plants cannot draw up moisture and if this continues for a prolonged period they will suffer. This is especially so for evergreens, which are then unable to replace the moisture they continue to lose through their leaves. You can still use smaller pots but fill them with the toughest plants, put them in the most sheltered spots and protect them among larger ones.

TIMBER

Easy to work with and (when obtained from ethical sources) sustainable, timber is a sympathetic material that can achieve a range of looks from the unapologetically formal to the relaxed and natural. Elegant, finial-adorned 'Versailles' (or 'Italianate') boxes, most often seen symmetrically paired at grand entrances and hosting topiary, are supremely stately. More humble are capacious, rustic half-barrels; the largest are a reasonable mid-term home for smaller trees and large shrubs. I'm not particularly enamoured of either, but I do have several trusty wooden window boxes and crates that are replanted often and given pride of place. I prefer a weathered finish to neatly painted, although environmentally sound garden timber paints offer a speedy and fun way of transforming basic or tired items.

A major advantage is that timber planters can be custom built (or home made) to fit awkward spaces. Boxes crafted from planed hard woods are refined and smart but are most successful as integral design features that remain in their original position, as they are not always easy to relocate. Troughs knocked together using reclaimed door panels, floorboards or skirting and displaying layers of peeling paint appeal to the shabby chic aesthetic, while silvered or bleached wood says 'seaside'. Raised beds, which are effectively non-portable, open-bottomed containers, are easily

ABOVE RIGHT Bamboo pipes are useful for displaying diminutive plants and trailers, and can be set at jaunty angles.

RIGHT Old wooden crates are of a handy shape and size for showing off mixed plantings of seasonal plants, including vegetables and herbs.

constructed from timber, whether using simple planks, logs still wearing bark or chunky railway sleepers.

The obvious downside to wooden containers is their limited life, and the care required to keep them in usable condition for as long as possible. Regular treatment with plant-friendly wood preservative or varnish will prolong their life, as will lining them with polythene or even butyl rubber – but be sure to punch plenty of drainage holes.

METAL

Whether cast, pressed, folded or welded, as a material for containers metal presents gardeners with a variety of distinct options: some flimsy and light, others durable and decidedly weighty. Ornamental lead planters, copper cauldrons and cast-iron urns honour tradition, while sheet steel is used to fabricate crisply precise, bang-up-to-date – even futuristic – products. Then there are the rugged agricultural and industrial offerings, including animal-feed troughs and galvanized water tanks.

Contemporary metal containers are more effective at housing foliage than flowers and are limited in their application. They are most purposeful when tailor made to complement architecture and integrated as permanent elements of a design. Stainless steel and aluminium will retain their reflective qualities long term and so are worthy of consideration for gloomy corners. Galvanized steel dulls down to a soft grey and appears at ease in any landscape. As a result of oxidization, many other metals become increasingly appealing over time: verdigris forms on copper and iron rusts. Corten – or 'weathering' – steel bears the same warm colouring as terracotta, courtesy of a deliberate rusty coat that develops protectively across its shiny surface within days of exposure to air and moisture. Readily available powder-coated zinc containers are a low cost, lightweight choice. My experience is that they rust through within a few years (so don't overstock with them, as I once did) and they are certainly not robust enough to be long-term homes for the likes of vigorous bamboos or evergreens.

More so than other substances, metals subject plant roots to extremes of temperature. In the hottest of days and in full sun they heat up considerably, potentially damaging delicate roots and drying out the compost. Equally, in winter, metal will provide little insulation from frost. Lining the inner walls with carpet offcuts or hessian sacking (although that will last only one season) will alleviate the problem.

ABOVE LEFT Corten or 'weathering' steel develops a decorative and protective rust coating within days of being exposed to air and moisture.

LEFT Containers made of metal range from the characterful and vintage (as here) to the highly finished and ultramodern.

STONE, RECONSTITUTED STONE AND CONCRETE

Containers carved from hewn lumps of natural stone are impressive, architecturally pleasing and emanate an air of permanence. In grand settings they look magnificent, though are sadly far beyond the average pocket and most gardens. But who needs them, when infinitely more affordable substitutes formed from reconstituted stone (particularly concrete) will weather to be – almost – indistinguishable? Genuine old stone sinks are highly sought after and the perfect home for dainty alpine plants; they, too, can be convincingly replicated using a mixture of coir (coconut fibre), sand and cement known as 'hypertufa'.

Thanks to their crisp architectural appearance and to the high-end finishes that can be achieved, concrete pots are gaining in popularity. Some reinforced concrete containers are akin to pieces of sculpture and this material can be turned into chic products. Buffed concrete presents an inviting surface that is fine-looking in modern and more traditional settings alike.

Handsome, tactile, polished marble planters and granite cubes suit unfussy planting and backgrounds but naturally command high prices. These too can be replicated: available in shades of grey, pink, green and white, terrazzo containers are composed of stone chips set in resin and polished to achieve a granite-like appearance. Made in moulds – which means they come in a variety of shapes including spheres – terrazzo is a hard-wearing alternative to marble and retails at a fraction of the price. Their clean, smooth lines are particularly at home in contemporary gardens, although mine integrate extremely well with more traditional pots in my collection.

Containers formed of stone or concrete are by their very nature durable and weather resistant. Weight is their major drawback: even the smallest examples can take some lifting. Site them carefully so that they won't need repositioning too often, or at all!

GLAZED

Earthenware pots coated in decorative glazes are eternal bestsellers. They represent excellent value because they are both produced in huge numbers (therefore keeping the cost down) and weather resistant (so long lived). They are also offered in the widest colour range of any material used to manufacture containers; an astonishing palette, in fact. Unlike terracotta, wood or metal they do not change appearance or discolour with age (although the glaze itself may craze) and are easily wiped clean: ideal for those not enamoured of patina or lichen.

Many of my own glazed pots I've had for thirty years or more and still I delight in them, although some I tired of quite quickly on account

ABOVE RIGHT Fashionable reinforced concrete planters are often handsome architectural statements.

RIGHT Durable glazed pots come in a variety of colours and finishes.

of their colour. I urge you to be colour cautious when choosing, as some of the brighter shades are too attention grabbing to be team players. Due to potential colour clashes, they may also restrict both the range of plants you can grow in them and the instances where you can use them. Two-tone and multiple-colour glazes can look great unplanted but may prove distracting and far from enhancing of any but the simplest plantings. Single colours are the safest visually, while neutral shades present greatest scope for planting and are the easiest to site and resite. All those longest in my service are finished in shades of green or brown. Paler colours are a good bet for lifting dull, shady areas, while especially dark finishes can be quite sombre-looking and must be carefully teamed with the right plants in a bright spot to be effective.

Because the glaze seals the surface of these containers, they are largely non-porous and so do not dry out as rapidly as unglazed earthenware, and sealing their bases with silicone allows them to be turned into water features.

IMPROVISED

All manner of objects can be co-opted to grow plants in. Seeking out unlikely vessels as homes for plants tests our inventiveness, stirs the imagination and is both fun and satisfying. One of the obvious draws is that, whether recycled, reclaimed or repurposed (or all three), improvised containers are usually free or inexpensive. Some may need adapting and require drainage holes to be added, while others are compost- and plant-ready. Buckets, bins, cooking pots, food tins, watering cans, teapots, colanders, crates, baths, water closets, cisterns, old boots and even offcuts of metal or plastic pipe are among the more obvious items that can be successfully transformed into leafy or flowery abodes. Some, such as wicker baskets and cans, might only last a season or two, but others that were intended to be long-serving in their previous capacity, including tin baths, dustbins and milk churns, will last on for many years in their new roles. Some finds are inevitably more successful and desirable than others and while the whackier receptacles – I'm thinking full-sized motor cars and washing machines – might guarantee comment, the more subtle are easier to integrate and live with longer term.

Antique metal items, including copper kettles (they look humorous hung in trees) and brass coal scuttles can be picked up surprisingly cheaply at auctions, as can agricultural salvage, such as feed troughs and galvanized buckets. Roughly made wooden pallet crates used to transport paving are ideal for trees or for mini raised allotment plots, and wooden crates are generally useful. Just keep your eyes peeled and your mind open!

ABOVE LEFT and LEFT Large or small, recycled tins are quirky and inexpensive homes for plants. If looked after, they can last several seasons before eventually rusting through.

LOOKALIKES AND SYNTHETICS

For most of us, charismatic containers shaped of lead or copper are prohibitively expensive. Fortunately, you can enjoy the look without breaking the bank using convincing mimics formed of manmade materials (complete with fake ageing), such as fibreglass or resin. Once planted, it's not particularly easy to distinguish the genuine article from the copy, and I have several faux lead planters that have been in faithful service for over twenty years; they regularly fool visitors. Lead lookalikes are stylish and radiate tradition, yet they sit comfortably in contemporary settings – perhaps due to their colouring and formal geometric patterning. Fibreglass is impermeable and containers made of it often lack pre-drilled drainage holes: as a result they can be instantly turned into attractive mini ponds. Being lightweight, fibreglass containers are ideal for balconies but, although weatherproof and durable, their surface is easily scratched so site them where they are not likely to be knocked. Some of the cheaper offerings are less believable and really not a fitting home to gorgeous plants, so only buy those that seduce you into believing they could be the real thing.

In recent years, consumer demand has prompted the development of more environmentally friendly substances, including 'fibreclay', which is a mixture of clay and wood pulp. It can be moulded into any shape, finished to authentically imitate almost any material from slate to weathered steel, and containers produced from it are affordable. Fibreclay is considerably heavier than fibreglass and so is very solid but equally easily scuffed and will chip if it is dropped. Although their longevity and durability continue to improve as new formulations and processes are developed, in my experience fibreclay containers have a limited life (of several years) so don't rely entirely on them. 'Fibrestone', which includes stone powder as part of its composite, lasts, on average, twice as long.

PLASTICS AND COVER-UPS

Containers formed of plastic are tough, inexpensive, long lasting and lightweight, and in those respects are an agreeable and practical proposition. Where looks are not the primary objective, such as for growing crops, this impermeable substance offers a very sensible option, especially as it also causes compost to dry out less quickly than most other materials. Environmentally and aesthetically, though, plastic is less than desirable and we are increasingly encouraged to limit its use in our gardens and elsewhere. Attempts by plastic manufacturers to simulate the likes of timber, stone and terracotta are often crude and even uglier than plastic that isn't pretending to be anything else. That said, this material does have a place in many gardens – even ornamentally. With holes drilled for drainage, plastic trug tubs (or Gorilla® tubs) make great planters for children, particularly as they come in many bright colours and various sizes and their handles make them easy to lift. For reasons

BLACK PLASTIC AND RECYCLING

If it were not for the advent of plastic pots, we would not enjoy the considerable modern convenience of buying plants of all sizes in full growth, at any time of year. Plant roots require the exclusion of light to develop well and black pots have been proven to be the optimum; many billions have been manufactured during the last few decades. But there has always been insufficient opportunity to recycle them and that has created a massive environmental issue. Sheds and garages all over the land are stuffed with difficult-to-pass-on used plastic pots and I've often had to politely decline 'donations' from friends and neighbours. Manufacturers have struggled to find an alternative as other more friendly substances have proved either too costly, too fragile or not to be as effective for growing strong, healthy specimens. However, there is, at last, hope of a solution, for pioneering members of the nursery industry are switching to taupe-coloured pots that are designed to be more readily recyclable, yet in trials, have still produced premium-quality plants. The tide is turning.

of weight or economy, plastic containers are sometimes the only option and, where necessary, it is easy to jazz them up or to disguise them.

Large black plastic pots with handles, such as those used by nurseries to grow specimen plants, are commodious homes for (small) trees and shrubs, and are considerably easier to shift around than terracotta, metal or timber containers of the same capacity. They can be masked by arranging other pots around them, or by encircling them with rolls of reed, willow or bamboo screening. Smaller plastic pots may be camouflaged in a variety of ways, from coiling with rope or wrapping in hessian sacking to sitting them inside timber boxes. For ease of removing them, plastic pots are also useful for potting temporary plants and putting them into more ornamental containers.

Ugly but efficient and lightweight plastic pots can be disguised in all manner of creative and inexpensive ways. These include using slate tiles, thin paving stones or lengths of reclaimed timber (such as skirting, floorboards or scaffold planks) screwed or glued together to box them in, whether singly or as collections.

ABOVE LEFT Pebble-filled wire baskets with a central void allow plants still in their original garden centre pots to be placed in for instant effect, and swapped readily when they begin to tire.

LEFT Here four matching clay roof tiles create a pot surround oozing rustic charm. They sit firmly on level surfaces and, simply wired together, can easily be dismantled.

PLANTING
FOR SUCCESS

PLANTING UP

PHOTOS AS A REFERENCE

Although gardening is an activity that helps us to disengage from technology, a certain advantage of mobile phone cameras is the ease with which you can take photographs of anything, anywhere. I'm now in the habit of snapping containers immediately after planting and at stages during their development. Glancing back through the images highlights just how much growth some plants can make in a season. That a few green blobs in a pot can very quickly become an eye-catching mass of colour never ceases to astonish. On the dull days of winter, looking through the snapshots is quite a tonic and they are invaluable when making creative plans for the growing season yet to come. They are a helpful reminder of successful plantings to use again and less triumphant ones to tweak or avoid in the future. I have tried and trusted combinations that are repeated most years but experimenting and trying out new plant associations is part of what makes container gardening so perpetually intoxicating.

The route to thriving planted containers involves unhurried preparation, quality components and diligent aftercare. There's nothing difficult or mysterious about growing plants in pots and once you've grasped the basics, the more advanced aspects of the subject will follow comfortably. It need be no more complicated than you make it. At its simplest you need one plant, a pot chosen to take into account the expected size and growth rate of that plant and fresh potting compost. Plus a little of your time, of course. That's how I started: that red rhododendron, an 'ornamental' plastic pot and a bag of ericaceous compost. More complex displays involve teaming plants that will live happily together in the same pot in terms of their cultural requirements and speed of growth, and which also complement each other aesthetically. Once planted, it's a case of watering as often as is needed and, less frequently, feeding and grooming.

Having gathered all that you need, you are ready to indulge in the immersive pleasure that is planting. It is not to be rushed. I find myself nattering (not too loudly!) to the plants as I'm potting and wishing them a long and healthy life. Although certain initial considerations may differ depending on whether you are planting for long or short term, the actual method of planting a container is the same whatever its size, shape or material, and whatever plants you are growing. The only significant variable is the quantity and configuration of the plants themselves. This chapter covers the practical side of container gardening and aims to help you understand the needs of your plants so they will flourish, and how to achieve displays that realize their full, deeply satisfying potential.

PREVIOUS PAGE With careful preparation and a bit of routine care, all manner of plants can be persuaded to put on a show in containers, from hardy grasses to tender climbing plants. Here thunbergia, hakonechloa and pennisetums informally intermingle.

LEFT Planting up

The compost

Plants draw all the water and nutrients required to sustain healthy growth via whatever medium they are planted into, and so it makes sense to use an optimum potting compost. An ideal mix includes fine particles with much coarser material to achieve an open-structured substrate that is well aerated and free draining, yet is also sufficiently moisture (and ideally nutrient) retentive. The quality of growing media is dependent on their raw ingredients, and on a well-balanced final blend. My experience of the cheapest products has rarely been a happy one – either for my plants or myself – and I've learnt that it is wise to pay the extra for a better grade.

A pot filled with compost is a contrived environment where the complex ecology and microscopic activity that is present in the ground is greatly reduced or even absent. Naturally, this lack of life has both drawbacks and advantages. At purchase, potting composts are devoid of micro-organisms and invertebrates, such as earthworms, that help aerate soil and maintain its structure. They also contain limited nutrients and trace elements, and so these must be replenished manually. On the plus side, processed compost should be free of the potential soil pests and diseases that are the reason it is inadvisable to use garden soil (unless sterilized) in pots. And it is far easier to mix bespoke compost to satisfy a particular plant than it is to alter the inherent qualities of your soil.

Proprietary growing media can be split into two basic groups: soil (or loam) based and soilless. Composts composed of mainly sterilized loam usually also contain grit or sand and mimic rich garden soil. However, they are very heavy (though ideal for balancing top-weighted plants, such as trees) and have a tendency to set hard, which can hinder watering. For these reasons, I never use soil-based compost neat.

Soilless composts are relatively lightweight and friable but, unless laced with a wetting agent (sometimes included in proprietary mixes) or moisture-retaining granules (see *Watering*, page 158), they are often tricky to re-wet if they dry out completely, which they are prone to do. I tend to use soilless compost only for single season displays. For anything more long term, in common with many other experienced container gardeners, I mix proprietary soilless compost with a trusted soil-based product and find this to be far more satisfactory than either on its own. The proportion of each depends on the plants. As soilless composts degrade more quickly and because loam composts are better at retaining nutrients, I increase the amount of loam for plants that I expect to remain in the same container for several years, but never to more than 50 per cent. I also recycle used compost – either by mixing it with fresh or in the lower half of larger containers – and see no harm in this, provided it isn't harbouring pests (such as vine weevil grubs) or fungal diseases like mildew.

CUSTOMIZING COMPOST

'Off the shelf' composts are generally cover-all 'multi-purpose' (also termed 'general' or 'all-purpose') or very specialized mixes sold in small quantities at high prices. Multi-purpose composts are easily customized to suit specific plants and it is cost effective to buy these ingredients separately and blend them yourself. Added bark chips or perlite improve structure and aeration; mixing in grit assists drainage; and there are various supplementary fertilizers and trace elements for long-term subjects, such as trees and shrubs. There are also watering aids that can be incorporated when potting (see *Watering*, page 158).

CROCKS OR NOT?

Recent trials have revealed that the traditional practice of adding a layer of very coarse material, such as crocks (pieces of broken pot), in the bottom of containers does not particularly assist drainage, as was previously believed. I've long been in two minds about using crocks myself because they can block essential drainage holes (leading to waterlogging), as well as create perfect hideouts for slugs, woodlice and adult vine weevils. However, most larger pots have wide or multiple drainage holes and, unless restricted in some way, some compost will inevitably wash through every time you water. Strategically arranging a few largish crocks (curved pieces are ideal) propped on each other over the holes is the best solution I know. Whether or not to use crocks is therefore really a matter of discretion, common sense and personal preference. The excess of broken pieces of terracotta that once always went below the compost, I now break up into smaller pieces and use as a surface mulch. Their sharp edges present an obstacle to snails but care should be taken when handling.

Even in this environmentally aware age and despite its being a precious non-renewable resource, the majority of soilless composts still contain a high percentage of peat. This is partly due to the fact that, even though they have been trialling a wide range of alternatives100 one hundred per cent viable replacement. Peat is simply an excellent substance for growing things in. So, as we are in a period of transition, many companies offer a compromise in the form of 'reduced peat' products. Even so, we must speed towards the point when we stop using peat altogether and cease destroying the wondrous and fragile landscapes from which it is obtained.

Currently available peat-free composts (aside from loam-based) are composed of mixed organic materials. These may include coir (coconut fibre), composted bark, woodchips and general green waste. Smaller amounts of inorganic materials such as grit, perlite (lightweight expanded volcanic glass) or mineral wool may also be incorporated. Some manufacturers are cagey about the contents but I always like to know what I'm using and have more confidence in those who openly declare their ingredients. Even with some of the long-standing peat substitutes, such as coir, there are fair-trade and carbon-footprint concerns, so compost producers are continually pushed to seek more 'local' materials. One manufacturer I've encountered produces bracken-based compost that also includes sheep's wool, which provides nitrogen and aids moisture-retention.

The off-the-peg, multi-purpose compost that I've recently switched to, and find very promising, is a blend of fine bark, wood fibre and coir – with added loam and fertilizer. It is endorsed by the Royal Horticultural Society and suits the majority of plants. The main exceptions are acid-loving rhododendrons and their kin, which require an ericaceous formula.

Long-term shrubs and trees

When growing trees, shrubs and other relatively long-lived plants in pots the usual intention is to keep them for several years or more. They are best potted individually (or if they are very slow-growing, maybe in a multiple of a single variety) rather than mixing them in the same container, as you might with short-term plants. I have several shrubs that have been with me for at least ten years and they are very important constants of my container displays. Taking into account this hoped-for longevity, consider the following future-proofing criteria before you pot.

First, select your pot with care. Make sure it is sound (I've had a pot fall apart just as I finished planting!) and is of a suitable size: most permanent plants require a container of generous dimensions and it is not desirable to have to repot large specimens too often. Remember also to avoid pots that are narrower at their opening than at any point further down. You may otherwise be unable to free an overgrown shrub without damaging it or its container. I've been there! Many of my own shrubs have been transferred to a larger pot at least once in their lifetime, although a few were housed promptly in very big pots and have remained so. There is no general rule for how capacious a pot you need, other than to ask advice when purchasing as the tolerances and growth rates of plants vary so much. Although they may initially look a bit lost, it makes sense to plant quick-growing shrubs directly into fairly large pots. Plants with fine root systems, such as camellias and rhododendrons, might languish if swimming in a vat of compost, so for these pick containers roughly two to three times the capacity of their original garden centre pots.

CONTINUED INTEREST

Achieving year-round interest is surprisingly easy, even using only a few pots. A permanently sited collection of evergreens and other plants that span much of the year with interest will also form a stable framework among which short-term plants may be added. As one season-specific plant fades, it can readily be removed and replaced so that the scene is ever looking its best and keeps you engaged throughout the year. You can scale up or down depending on season and your own schedule. Well-chosen permanent plants will hold their appeal even if the casual pots are absent.

Drilling drainage holes

Pot feet

POT DRESSING

In pots, mulching, or covering the surface of the compost with a layer of loose material, whether organic or inert, is primarily a very decorative finishing touch. Practically, mulches also assist moisture retention, helping to keep roots and compost cooler and reducing evaporation in hot weather. Because it excludes light, a mulch will also inhibit germination of weed seeds and makes any that break through easier to pull out. Ornamental mulches are appropriate mainly for longer-term plantings where the soil surface would otherwise remain unattractively on show. In more temporary displays the plants themselves usually fill out to cover all. For a co-ordinated and coherent look, choose a material that complements both plant and pot – pebbles and slate chips are both universally effective. Although not the most aesthetically appealing, commercially available mineralized straw is an organic mulch that is very efficient at weed control and has some effect as a slug and snail

repellent. There is, however, one major drawback with mulching: because the compost surface is no longer on view or readily accessible, it can make judging when to water even trickier. If you are not a confident waterer, then either don't mulch at all or restrict it to a few key plants.

Quite often it's simply a case of visually balancing pot and plant so they look comfortably in proportion.

Never plant a pot that has no drainage holes: choose those with a large central hole (30mm/1¼in plus in diameter) or several smaller ones (8mm/½in plus), or drill some using a bit suited to the material of the container. Turn the pot upside down and take all the necessary safety precautions to prevent damaging it or yourself. Use a tile bit for ceramics and terracotta and a grinding stone drill bit to enlarge the holes where necessary. Ideally, also raise pots marginally off the ground so there is a small gap between them and the surface below. This will allow excess moisture to drain through freely. Use pot feet, flat stones, bricks or chunks of timber. Plant large pots *in situ* and site them carefully as, when planted, they can be very difficult to manoeuvre.

Finally, if using a porous container such as terracotta – and especially if it is to be sited in an exposed or very sunny spot where it may dry out more rapidly – an option that reduces moisture loss is lining the sides with an old compost bag. This also makes it easier to get plants out when repotting.

And now you are all set for planting!

With care, slow-growing *Pinus sylvestnis* 'Chantry Blue' will thrive in a medium-sized container for several years before requiring a larger pot or planting out.

A potful of summer climbers

For short-term or seasonal displays that might last for months rather than years you can combine a variety of plants in the same pot to create a living arrangement. These form a display in their own right but can also be teamed with pots of longer-term plants for a more varied and balanced picture. Here I'm planting thunbergia and *Ipomoea lobata*: both are fast-growing climbing plants, usually treated as annuals (see also pages 82–83).

1 It is vital for healthy growth that compost drains freely, so ensure there are adequate drainage holes in the bottom of your container. When compost becomes waterlogged, root systems may be damaged and plants will struggle. An optional few pieces of broken terracotta pot or flattish stones in the bottom will prevent compost seeping out. (See *Crocks or not?*, page 147.)

2 Whilst large pots are best planted *in situ*, smaller easily transportable ones may be established in a more sheltered spot before being moved to prominence. Begin filling with compost, firming gently as you go. Never over-firm, as this expels air and can impede root growth. If using small plants, as is usually the case with summer containers, fill with compost to within 15cm (6in) of the container's top edge. You can always add a bit or scoop some out depending on the size of the plants you are using.

Most proprietary composts include only four to six weeks' worth of fertilizer. Thereafter, it's over to you – use either a general soluble or liquid feed when watering, or add controlled-release fertilizer in granular form to the compost when planting (see *Feeding*, page 160). At the same time, mix in water-storing granules (at the rate recommended on the packet) – these swell up like a gel and hold moisture for roots to tap into when required (see *Watering*, page 158).

③ Although you can buy very elaborate ornamental supports for climbing plants, because they will mostly be hidden, I usually opt for a simple wigwam of thin hazel, birch or lime branches (or, in their absence, bamboo canes). For a 50cm/20in diameter pot, use five or six branches, evenly spaced around the edge. If you wish, for extra support add some finer, twiggier branches or weave pliable stems horizontally.

④ Tie the branches together at the top with garden jute or raffia. As a decorative finishing touch, particularly when using bamboo canes, I top off with a spherical finial made by tightly wrapping garden string round and over itself until it forms a neat ball. This takes a few minutes but is worth the time and effort.

⑤ Water all plants in their pots beforehand: never plant them dry. Arrange the two types of climber

alternately, positioning one plant per main upright, a few centimetres in from the edge. Especially if they are dense or matted together, tease out some of the roots to encourage them to spread quickly into fresh compost. Fill up with more compost (with additives from step 3) so that the finished level is around 5cm/2in below the rim. Don't overfill, as this

will cause water to run off rather than to seep down to the roots. Firm gently before watering thoroughly.

⑥ Weave the twining stems on to the supports and, if necessary, loosely tie the stems with jute or raffia – or clip with sweet pea rings – to get them started. Thereafter, they will mostly wind their own way, needing only occasional guidance.

Bath thymes

With planning, you can cram a selection of culinary herbs that delight eyes, nose and taste buds into a space less than a metre square. Most herbs grow rapidly and, when planted together, not only will they compete for food and water, but the less vigorous kinds will be crowded out by the stronger growers. To give each a fair chance, plant them individually into terracotta pots of varying size and arrange these in a larger container. This old tin bath is ideal and has served as my herb garden for many years. Positioned in full sun, it has provided a constant spring-and-summer supply of fresh parsley, sage, rosemary, chives, coriander, basil and various different thymes (see overleaf). In this version, thymes are the focus: they are such good-looking, obliging little plants, and even many of the variegated varieties, such as pink-flowered 'Silver Posie', can be used in the kitchen. All manner of other plants, including succulents, alpines and dwarf bulbs, also suit being shown off in this way.

❶ Containers not originally intended to house plants usually do not have drainage holes so drill several of at least 1cm/½in diameter in the bottom and raise off the ground on large flat stones, bricks or pot feet to allow excess water to drain out. Pot each herb into a terracotta pot that allows it room to grow. As an option, place a few broken crocks or terracotta shards in the bottom to stop compost washing through.

❷ Many herbs such as rosemary, thyme and sage are native of Mediterranean regions and so thrive in full sun and soil that drains freely. Mixing fine horticultural grit with standard multi-purpose compost both improves aeration and aids drainage. A small amount of controlled-release fertilizer will provide enough nutrients for one growing season.

3 Most herbs are obligingly easy to propagate and so overgrown plants are inexpensive to replace. Thymes and mints, for example, can be readily split. Trim the plants back – lightly in the case of thymes and heavily for mints – then tap out of their pots. Carefully tease the plants apart – first into two and then into smaller pieces. A knife may be necessary for mint!

4 Pot a strong, well-rooted division of mint or thyme back into the original pot and keep a couple of others as spares. Thymes are also easy from cuttings – as are rosemary, sage and hyssop. Sow seeds of parsley, basil and coriander in spring and early summer. Top off with an ornamental, slug-deterring layer of grit.

5 As your plants will not root deeply into the bath itself, you can save compost and make it less weighty by filling up the bottom third or so with lightweight material, such as upturned plastic pots or trays (they have to be useful for something). Then add compost before arranging your potted herbs. Stand some pots high and sink others lower to create a pleasing contour.

KEEPING YOUR HERBS LOOKING MINT

The great convenience of growing herbs in a collected-together yet segregated style is that you can keep your display looking its best by swiftly lifting out tired or congested plants and replacing them with fresh. You can split and repot those you take out, bring in substitutes waiting in the wings or add something new from a nursery or garden centre. You are also able to regulate watering and give each plant more or less depending on its thirstiness. Picking your herbs regularly will help keep them tidy and in good shape, besides enhancing your cooking.

CARING FOR
PLANTS IN POTS

Unlike plants growing in the ground that, once established, should be largely able to fend for themselves, plants in containers rely heavily on us. I liken them to animals kept as pets: as 'captives' they are totally dependent on their keepers for their basic needs of food and water. If you adopt that psyche you'll be on the right track.

In addition to essential watering and feeding, depending on their type and habit, your plants may need trimming, tidying, repotting, winter protection and occasionally rescuing from infestations of pests or disease.

By choosing easier-to-care-for plants that are perhaps not too vigorous, are disease resistant or are resilient and winter hardy, it is possible to reduce the required amount of tending. Unless you have the time and mindset, it defeats the aim if so much maintenance is called for that you become enslaved to your plants. In spring especially, it is all too easy to get carried away buying plants or sowing seed, only to find later that you have more than you can reasonably look after. Given time, you'll find that happy balance between having enough planted pots to keep you engaged and not so many that caring for them becomes difficult. It makes far more sense to have a few really well looked after pots than dozens that receive insufficient individual attention. One ruse I've learnt is to group a few containers that require minimal maintenance with just one or two that are more labour-intensive. This way you can concentrate your efforts on the latter whilst enjoying a complete and varied picture.

These next few pages are an introduction to the key aspects of aftercare, most of which are very necessary to maintaining a healthy, good-looking display. For me, the interaction with plants when dead-heading, pruning or checking they are in good health is integral to my enjoyment of gardening, and I find it calming.

Watering

Watering is the one vital aspect of container gardening that is potentially a major chore. You cannot sidestep it. Plants will struggle on indefinitely when hungry (although they may look increasingly sickly) but left thirsty for very long and they'll really suffer. Ultimately, they'll give up. Some more quickly than others. The length of time a plant can survive in dry compost depends on what it is: annuals with very soft growth won't last more than a few days, if that. Many hardy shrubs and trees will, as I've discovered, cling on for weeks or even months. Some perennials and most bulbs will lie dormant and bounce back once their moisture supply returns. But the aim, of course, is not to stress your plants and to give them water when they need it. In pots, overwatering can be as much an issue as underwatering and so understanding how and when to water is crucial. This is not rocket science, but it can be time-consuming, and deciding if a plant needs water is sometimes tricky – even for seasoned gardeners. If you take it in your stride, though, and you've not given yourself the difficulty of too many pots, watering is therapeutic and relaxing.

Once properly rooted out, plants in the soil should no longer require manual watering – except in extreme conditions – as their roots are able to seek moisture. In a pot this ability is curbed and, especially where the compost surface is completely hidden, only after a prolonged heavy spell might sufficient rain have filtered through. Clearly, compost doesn't dry out as quickly in cool weather or when plants are not growing actively, or in shade. On a hot, windy day, though, a pot packed with annuals on a south-facing terrace will likely need watering at least twice. In summer especially, water at the cooler ends of the day to limit evaporation.

With experience, you'll be able to spot instantly when a plant is desperate for water, or is too wet: wilting is the primary symptom of both. The easiest decider is to push a finger deep into the compost to check for moisture. If the pot is not too large, another test is simply to lift it to see if it weighs particularly light or heavy. That the surface is dry does not necessarily mean that the compost further down is also, and so both tests help in determining whether or not to water when checking routinely.

ABOVE RIGHT Even though a shower may refresh them, all but a heavy and prolonged downpour is unlikely to reach the roots of plants with dense canopies that project beyond the width of their pots. Hand watering is usually still required.

RIGHT An automatic drip irrigation is useful if you have a lot of pots.

SAVVY WATERING TIPS

- Collect as much rainwater as possible from every available surface. There are some excellent rain harvesting systems that ensure not a drop is wasted.

- Especially in the heat of summer, leave filled watering cans around for convenience and wilting plant emergencies.

- The quickest way to re-wet smaller pots that have dried out totally is to plunge them in a large bucket until bubbles stop appearing. Alternatively, stand them in a tray of water until they have revived.

- Water slowly but thoroughly. A fast flood of water is more likely to cascade over the sides and not seep properly to the roots where it is needed.

- Add water-storing gel when planting as this provides back up moisture for roots to draw on if you are a haphazard waterer.

- As a rule, larger pots, unless completely congested with roots, will need less frequent watering than smaller.

- Sit particularly thirsty plants in saucers or trays. Moisture will be drawn up through the compost in a capillary action, but don't leave constantly standing in water.

When it comes to how to water, the main thing to grasp is that it's the roots that drink, and therefore water should be aimed efficiently in their direction rather than over the rest of the plant. Water thoroughly so that the compost is saturated. A superficial sprinkling may barely penetrate the surface. The compost should not remain constantly soggy, though, as this can cause the roots to rot, so do not water indiscriminately. All containers must have holes in the base to allow excess water to drain away, and larger ones should ideally be raised slightly off the ground on pot feet. Unless it is escaping down the insides because the compost is resisting being rewetted after drying out completely, once water starts trickling through the drainage holes the job is done.

When watering a large number of pots, it makes sense to use a hosepipe. I seldom bother with a nozzle as they can be too forceful and a challenge to direct only towards the compost. I tend not to have the tap turned on at full pressure as applying the water more slowly ensures it sinks deep. If only a few pots need water (not all will dry out at the same rate), I'll reach for a watering can: I keep two or three strategically placed and ready-filled with rainwater. It is generally easier to pour and less wasteful if you remove the rose from the end of the spout. An exception is when watering freshly planted containers as the gentler, more even flow helps settle plants in without washing out any compost. An advantage of using a can rather than a hose is that you can gauge more easily how much water you are giving each container. Some of my larger pots require two or three large canfuls (20–30 litres) each: I pour on one canful and give it a few minutes to soak in before returning with the next. Slowly and methodically is the most assured way to water.

If your time is limited, there are ways of lessening the amount of hand watering required. Drip irrigation systems adhere to the 'slow' principle and are particularly useful if you have many large pots. They consist of a main hose from which spring any number of smaller arterial pipes fitted with nozzles that drip or seep rather than spray water. They can be automated on a timer so are helpful if you go away. Water-storing gels are supplied as a sugar-like substance that swells up to 400 times its own weight in water and can be mixed with compost at planting time. This provides a useful moisture source for roots to tap into but it is not a substitute for watering. Be careful not to exceed the recommended dose as too much can create a medium that is permanently damp and difficult for young plants to root into.

Feeding

Like all living things plants need food as well as water to flourish. Most multi-purpose composts contain only a four to six week supply of fertilizer and this may be washed through more rapidly with frequent watering. Thereafter, plants confined to containers will go hungry unless you provide for them. Ready-made fertilizers contain the vital nutrients of nitrogen (N), phosphorus (P) and potassium (K) in varying proportions, along with much tinier quantities of other elements, including manganese, iron and magnesium. The ratio of the three 'macronutrients' is declared on proprietary fertilizers as 'N-P-K'. The amount of each included in a product depends on its intended use. Nitrogen is essential for healthy leaves, phosphorus aids root development, whilst potassium assists flower and fruit production, as well as contributing to overall resilience and vigour. Tomato fertilizers, for instance, contain relatively high levels of potassium and that is why many gardeners, including myself, also use them to boost flowering plants. Homemade comfrey 'tea' is also potassium-rich: it is easy to produce in just six weeks or so and is, of course, wholly organic. Nettles and borage produce a feed that is more nitrogenous. Chicken manure (available as pellets) is another excellent source of nitrogen and liquid seaweed extract is a plant super-tonic that stimulates all-round healthy growth and is an ingredient of many general fertilizers, both organic and inorganic.

Whilst my preference is for organic, inorganic compounds composed of mined minerals or synthetic chemicals are more fast-acting. I rely on them to help sustain rapid-developing seasonal plants that produce a large amount of growth and flowers on relatively small root systems, or are crowded together and so quickly use up nutrients. These are available as liquid or powder concentrates that should be diluted or dissolved following the manufacturers' instructions. The enhanced performance of plants fed in this way is very noticeable.

By far the most effortless method of feeding container plants is to incorporate a controlled-release granular fertilizer at planting time, although these are also non-organic. They release nutrients gradually through the growing season when the compost temperature and moisture levels are sufficiently high, but slow down when it is colder and plants are less active. They can also be applied each spring as a topdressing to feed longer-term plants.

ABOVE Controlled-release fertilizer is a very useful aid that can be mixed with the compost at planting time or sprinkled on annually. Your plants are then kept fed over many months as the granules dissolve slowly through the growing season.

Deadheading, trimming & tidying

ABOVE Removing dead flowers from most annuals and tender perennials (here osteospermums) keeps plants neat and encourages new buds.

ABOVE Trim away old or damaged leaves to keep plants looking their best and reduce the risk of them developing diseases such as mildew.

Planted containers tend to be granted prominent positions in our gardens and so it makes sense to keep them looking their best for as long as possible. The amount of maintenance, in addition to essential watering and feeding, varies depending on the type of plant. Long-term trees and shrubs may require relatively little routine care other than removal of damaged leaves and stems, and pulling out weeds. Some will be better for pruning or trimming to keep them neat and within bounds, and evergreens may need an occasional shake to help shed older, yellowing leaves.

Colourful short-term displays, especially summer containers packed with floriferous annuals and tender perennials, often involve more effort. The regular removal of faded flowers is primarily a cosmetic exercise but will also encourage some plants to bloom for longer by delaying them in reaching their ultimate goal of producing seed. Some newer cultivars are bred to be sterile (although they may still produce nectar for bees) and will bloom tirelessly in a futile attempt to reproduce. In others, such as pelargoniums and begonias, if blooms are left to decompose on the plant, especially in wet weather, they may rot and spread fungal diseases. For the same hygiene reasons, pick off and clear up damaged, diseased and part-chewed leaves as you spot them and prune out dead or dying stems and shoots. If you enter into the spirit and do it little and often, you ought to find this a satisfying time-out activity. Usually, spent flowers should be nipped off individually with stalks, but for certain plants it's the entire flower head or spike that is removed. Some, such as violas and petunias, are easy to pinch out between finger and thumb whilst others, including dahlias and roses, require scissors or secateurs. For those that produce their flowers in flushes, including argyranthemums and nemesias, it is easier to sheer over the whole plant. If cut back hard after flowering, a wide variety of hardy perennials, including hardy geraniums, tiarellas and brunneras, will reward you with a crop of fresh leaves, if not also more blooms. Particularly vigorous plants may need trimming or thinning out as they develop to allow other less strong growers in the same container opportunity to establish, whilst pinching out the growing tips of young plants encourages them to bush out.

Such diligent micromanagement isn't the most desirable treatment for all plants, though. Most grasses, a host of hardy perennials and many annuals fade with style and grace (see page 98) and left will offer up winter structure, a cold season larder for birds and shelter for insects.

Repotting & rejuvenating

When a plant is pot-bound the root system can no longer function properly because, relative to the mass of roots, there is insufficient compost to hold moisture or nutrients. Telltale signs include poor growth, yellowing leaves, matted surface roots, readily wilting young shoots and roots growing out from the drainage holes. Ideally you'll be on the case before any of your plants become desperate, but repotting sizeable plants is something most of us tend to avoid for as long as possible. Due to weight, cost or other factors, it's not always practical to move plants on into ever-larger containers. Fortunately, the majority of shrubs and trees will respond well to judicious root-pruning, thus affording them a new lease of life without going up a pot size. If you are prepared to do this every couple of years, it is possible to keep many shrubs to a manageable size – and in the same pot – for a very long while.

Large pot-bound shrubs can offer considerable resistance when it comes to evicting them, so water thoroughly to soften up the compost and tip the pot on its side in order to get a better grip. Trim off roots protruding from the drainage hole and, if necessary, slide the blade of an old handsaw down inside to loosen the roots. Lining the container with old compost bags when potting gives you something to tug at and prevents roots from adhering themselves to the rough inner walls of the pot. When potting back into the same container, tease out the roots and shake off most of the old compost. Loosen the root ball with your fingers and use a strong jet of water to wash away any remaining soil. Up to 30 per cent of the roots can be pruned away but the aim is to cut out a few whole sections of root rather than a general trim of the entire root ball, as this would remove all the vital finer roots. It is often wise to lightly prune the top growth to compensate for the hacking of the roots. Repot using entirely fresh compost, occasionally tapping the pot sides to help the compost filter in among the roots (this is easier if you use compost that is not too wet) and water thoroughly to settle it. As a rule, keep the plant at the same level as previously – do not be tempted to bury more deeply. Ideally, provide protection from heat and drying winds whilst the roots are re-establishing.

Overgrown clumps of perennials, such as hostas, persicaria, geraniums and heucheras, are easy and satisfying to deal with. Tip out and divide them in spring and pot some of the healthiest divisions back into the same container using fresh compost.

ABOVE Many shrubs, including Japanese maples, will likely need transferring to a large container after a few years. To keep them going in a container they appear to have outgrown, carefully root-prune and repot using fresh compost.

ABOVE RIGHT Protect cold-vulnerable plants such as tree ferns (dicksonia species) that may be too large to manoeuvre under cover with an insulating layer of horticultural fleece.

RIGHT I use vintage sack trucks to move heavier pots and I sometimes display them with the pots!

Wrapping up in winter

Inevitably you'll gather some plants that aren't hardy enough to stay outdoors through the winter and must be protected in some way from cold and wet. Some, such as tender perennial bedding plants, are more cost effective to replace each year than to store, whilst others such as tree ferns are too precious to leave to chance.

Winter protection is really a matter of common sense, so keep an eye on the weather forecast and especially night-time temperatures. My pots are moved in relays according to hardiness so that the display isn't stripped bare overnight, and a whole variety of protective measures are employed. Some plants such as succulents and shrubby tender perennials are moved into the greenhouse and polythene tunnel (a few choice succulents and coleus are afforded room in the house), some into cold frames, some such as dahlias and cannas are cut back, dried off and stored in the (frost-free) shed or garage. Others remain *in situ* but are moved together to protect each other or wrapped with horticultural fleece or sacking. Huddled together in a group, larger pots will offer smaller ones a degree of protection and if particularly bad weather is forecast you can wrap them up or move them to a more sheltered spot until conditions improve.

LIFTING AND MOVING POTS

It's not difficult to find yourself with at least one or two pots that, especially when filled with compost, are very heavy indeed. Moving them may be near impossible without assistance and some kind of equipment or ingenuity. I've had to move my pots around and transport them full very many times and they are rearranged regularly. Most are purposely very manageable but occasionally one of my heftier pots has to be relocated and that's when I wheel out my vintage sack trucks. They are as good looking as they are practical but modern versions are readily available at reasonable cost and those that can be converted to lie flat like a trolley are doubly useful. An old blanket wrapped around the sides will protect pots from damage. An alternative are mini pot trolleys on castors. They are not especially attractive but are very useful for large containers, allowing you to shunt them around easily, and can be hidden by smaller pots in groups.

FRIEND OR FOE?

Bumblebee

Comma butterfly nectaring on *Echinacea* 'White Swan'

LEFT Peacock butterfly on nemesia

In tending the land – even if it's just a tiny territory in a pot – growers and gardeners have the opportunity to assist many creatures, in particular bees, hoverflies, butterflies and other vital pollinating insects, facing difficult times. Great pleasure can come from respectful interaction with nature and we must be ever more mindful in our approach.

The majority of creatures that inhabit or visit our gardens cause no harm. Most are beneficial, while those that cause significant damage to plants form a tiny minority. With a few exceptions, the latter are fairly easy to deal with – especially if detected early – and because we are usually in closer contact with plants growing in containers, pests and diseases affecting them are more easily spotted.

There's a balance in nature that isn't easy to achieve in a small garden and barely possible within the confines of containers – unless they are planted primarily and ingeniously for wildlife – and so manual intervention is occasionally necessary. In all but a few instances, although time-consuming and intensive, the best remedy is to pick off the offending creatures and/or affected plant parts. Be philosophical: isolated attacks or outbreaks can be treated with equanimity as part and parcel of having a garden. Consider also that what we may deem as pests, especially many invertebrates, are part of the food chain and therefore comprise the diets of many more welcome creatures. The ideal, therefore, is not to totally eradicate these 'pests' but reduce or control their numbers. The range of fauna, as well as flora, is essential for biodiversity and a healthy environment, so catering for desirable predators in this way aids the local ecology.

POLLINATOR POTS

To give pollinating insects plenty of choice and to ensure they roam as much of the garden as possible, I plant all my containers with them in mind and try to span as much of the year as possible. For maximum patronage, pollinator pots are best positioned in sheltered, sunny places, using plants that offer a succession of flowers over as long a period as possible. Bumblebees possess an inherent preference for purplish flowers and, along with pink, yellow and orange, butterflies favour them also. Single blooms are always preferable to over-engineered doubles as the extra sets of petals make it harder for them to access pollen and nectar. If possible, group pots together to concentrate their signals to insects.

A few undesirables

Vine weevil larvae

Aphids – blackfly

Lily beetle

VINE WEEVIL

No greater nuisance is there to container gardeners than the brown-headed, off-white grubs of these beetle-like creatures. The grubs overwinter in the compost and generally emerge as adults in late spring. The adults are nocturnal so you are likely to encounter them only if inspecting plants at night. Adults do less direct damage than the grubs, which destroy plants by gnawing their roots and fleshy crowns or tubers. Often you won't realize there's a problem until the top of the plant completely wilts and becomes detached from what remains of its roots. The grubs feed on fleshy-rooted plants, like heucheras, cyclamen, succulents and begonias. To control them, order nematodes on the internet for spring or early autumn, when the compost is the right temperature (not below 5°C/41°F).

SNAILS (AND SLUGS)

I wish snails didn't cause such damage. If only they were content to devour one whole leaf rather than nibbling a few unsightly holes in many! Far more often than slugs, which most often feed nearer ground level, snails climb to find food. Growing in containers gives you an advantage but these beautiful creatures will seek them out unless sated with a more ready and plentiful supply elsewhere. Where plants are touching they may cunningly climb from one to the other to reach their meal, so isolate the more vulnerable. There are very many possible deterrents and controls but no single method is efficient, so simultaneously employ as many as possible. I've had some success with copper tape, raising targeted plants up high and homemade garlic solution sprayed on leaves and stems.

APHIDS

Especially prevalent in spring and summer when they infest the new shoots, buds and leaf undersides of a whole host of plants, sap-sucking aphids (blackfly, greenfly and other colours) reproduce rapidly, particularly in hot, dry conditions. Sap sucking spreads viruses and weakens or distorts the plant. Aphids also secrete a sticky honeydew, which may cause sooty mould on leaves. Wipe or pick off small colonies or spray with soft soap. They are a major food source for native predators including ladybirds and lacewings. Most aphids cannot fly but when a plant becomes too crowded or weakened, the next generation is born with wings and will migrate to a new host.

ANTS

Ants very occasionally nest in large containers and are not necessarily harmful to plants (although they do farm and protect aphids whose honeydew they covet). However, I've occasionally had a problem where they've mined around the roots, displacing compost, and created voids that affect the health and vigour of plants. If a plant appears to be struggling and you notice ants around the pot, tip it out and wash away as much of the compost, as well as ants and eggs, as you can before repotting with fresh soil.

LILY BEETLE

Specific to lilies (lilium) and fritillaries (fritillaria), these brilliant orange-red beetles rapidly devour leaves. However, their colour renders them easy to spot and individually pick off. They can be present from late March through until autumn. You'll rarely see more than a few at a time, but more generally appear within a day or two so check plants often. They can be less easy to find again if accidentally knocked to the ground so put some card at the base of plants to catch them. They can fly but seem to keep this ability in reserve. Orange eggs are laid on the undersides of leaves and the similarly coloured larvae hide out in a layer of black slime, usually underneath the lower leaves. Scrape them off or remove them complete with the leaf.

LEAF MINER

Leaf miners are common and are the larvae of many sorts of beetles, moths and flies. Their name comes from their burrowing between the layers of leaf tissue. They are particularly prevalent on certain plants including chrysanthemums, argyranthemums and nasturtiums. Although they make leaves look unsightly, with their meandering trails that show brown or white on the leaves' surfaces, they are not harmful to the plant's health. Pick off mined leaves.

THRIPS

Barely visible to the naked eye, these sap-sucking insects tend to be specific to particular plant species. I've experienced real difficulty with gladiolus thrip – especially as they can overwinter on the corms. If left unchecked they can seriously scar and disfigure plants to the point that they are not worth keeping. Organic sprays, such as natural pyrethrum, fatty acids or plant oils, can give some control but these have a very short persistence and so will require reapplication to be effective.

SCALE INSECT

These tiny blister-like brown or straw-coloured sap-sucking insects cluster on the stems and leaf veins of shrubby evergreens, including sweet bay, citrus and camellias. They secrete a sticky honeydew which drips on to leaves below and causes a black sooty mould to form. This is often more noticeable than the insect itself. Small infestations can be satisfyingly but time-consumingly scraped off. In severe cases, prune off affected parts and growth or dispense with the plant to prevent them spreading to others.

CATERPILLARS AND OTHER LARVAE

The term 'caterpillar' refers specifically to the larvae of butterfly and moth species, very few of which damage garden plants to great extent. Notable exceptions include Small and Large White butterflies – the 'Cabbage Whites' – which, as their name suggests, feed mainly on brassicas. I grow nasturtiums especially for them and transfer across any eggs or caterpillars spotted on other plants. Some moth larvae feed on specific genera – the mullein moth attacks verbascum and the box-tree moth is a devastating pest affecting box plants that has only recently arrived in the UK. Sawfly larvae look similar to caterpillars and can completely defoliate host plants. They are, however, limited to certain genera such as gooseberries, roses and geraniums.

WOODLICE

Congregations of these grey armoured creatures are an expected sight if you lift a pot, although they quickly disperse when disturbed. Diet-wise they are mainly concerned with debris and are performing a beneficial clean-up job. Sometimes I've noticed, though, that they will move in and continue devouring the leaves of hostas already decimated by snails. They can also home in on seedlings but it is rare for them to cause a major problem. For the most part just let them go about their business.

RATS, MICE AND SQUIRRELS

Spring-flowering bulbs, especially crocuses and tulips, are a target for rodents. In pots, the only effective way I've found of outwitting them is to lay chicken wire buried in the top of the compost just below the rim.

A few of the welcome

Frog

Ladybird larva

Lacewing

FROGS, TOADS AND NEWTS

These three amphibians are gardeners' aides. The common frog is widely distributed and is resident in many gardens, especially those with ponds. Frogs are most active at night and hibernate during the winter under piles of rotting leaves, logs or rocks. They are well known and respected for feasting on small slugs, snails and other invertebrates. With a similar diet to frogs, common toads are also widespread in this country and live away from water, except when they are mating. They usually grow larger than frogs and are distinguished by their warty rather than smooth skin. The smooth newt is common in the UK but is a protected species. On land it eats small invertebrates.

HOVERFLIES

Hoverflies are perfectly described in their common name: they often hover awhile in mid-air in between bouts of nectar collecting from a variety of flowers: mostly those with flat, open centres on which they can land easily. At first glance, some look similar to bees but are easily distinguished by the shape of their much larger eyes. Drone flies (*Eristalis tenax*) are the most common and widespread of the 250 or so UK species. I find them fascinating and calming to watch and photograph. Around 50 per cent of species of these important pollinating insects have larvae that devour aphids in quantity.

BEES

The decline in numbers of many species of these vital pollinators is a matter of alarm for gardeners and food producers alike. We must keep encouraging them into our gardens and aid them as much as possible. The collective hum of bees buzzing as they collect pollen on a warm day in midsummer is one of the most uplifting sounds – and sights – imaginable. There are over 250 wild bee species in the UK: 25 are bumblebees (bombus species) and just two are honeybees (apies species). All avoid blooms that are dense or complicated to penetrate and are most heavily attracted to flowers of yellow, purple and blue. The most common bumblebees are the buff-tailed, red-tailed and common carder. Honeybees are much smaller and less hairy. There are some very useful printed identification charts available to help determine the less common.

LADYBIRDS

Both adults and larvae feed voraciously on aphids, homing in on infected plants. In their lifetime a single ladybird can eat up to 5,000 aphids and so are one of the best possible controls. Harlequins, which originated in southeast Asia and have up to nineteen spots, can look similar first glance to UK native species. However, these are a larger invasive species that put our native ladybirds at risk by out-competing for food and preying on the eggs and larvae of our native two- and seven-spot species.

LACEWINGS

These slender, delicate-looking pollinating insects, with long either green or brown bodies and transparent, fairy-like wings, are seldom seen in large number but may be spotted flitting singly during the day or, more often, discreetly at dusk. Both adults and larvae devour aphids – one larva can eat two hundred a week. The larvae of some species go into camouflage by placing sucked-out aphid skins among the bristles on their upper surface.

HEDGEHOGS

The hedgehog population in Britain has halved since the Millennium. Destruction of hedgerows and a consequent reduction of their invertebrate food source, as well as an increase in badger numbers (their only significant predator), are among the many culprits. There is a glimmer of hope that hedgehogs are beginning to prosper again in urban gardens, so do everything you can to assist. They take shelter under piles of leaves and wood and hibernate through winter so leave an undisturbed, not over-tidied corner for them. Also provide them a way in and out of your garden as they will roam many hectares a night for food.

BEETLES

Ground and rove beetles are the commonest of the 1,300 or so native British species and can often be spotted scuttling away if you move a stone, a leaf or a pot. They live in or on the soil and both adults and larvae eat a wide variety of insects, slugs and other invertebrates. Encourage them by leaving small piles of leaf litter.

BIRDS

Some species may be less than appreciated on the veg plot but otherwise birds are extremely welcome and very engaging garden visitors. They are enthralling to watch as they go about their business, which includes picking off aphids, caterpillars and various grubs. A friendly robin or two frequents almost every garden and they have a habit of turning up when they think there's a meal in the offing. Whenever I unearth vine weevil or other grubs, I spread them out on a table or paving: they are soon scooped up, not wasted. Let dealing with undesirables become a positive experience!

BUTTERFLIES AND MOTHS

I had to include butterflies here as their presence in our gardens is wholly spirit-lifting and they are equally as beautiful, if not more so, as the blooms they frequent. Ecologically they are an important part of the food chain and reliable indicators of the health of the wider environment. They are not such efficient pollinators as bees and hoverflies but they inevitably transfer pollen as they flit from flower to flower seeking nectar. Moths are important night pollinators and the staple diet of bats, although some more colourful species such as the hummingbird hawk-moth and garden tiger are day-flying.

Common carder bumblebee (*Bombus pascuorum*) and honeybee (*Apies mellifera*)

Robin

Painted Lady butterfly

Organic pest control

Ever-tightening laws and legislation mean the range of synthetic chemicals available to gardeners has decreased considerably in recent years, and rightly so. Thankfully, the days when amateur growers were responsible for heavy, and sometimes indiscriminate, use of chemicals is long gone. Not before time and much damage has already occurred. I shamefully admit that in days long past I was guilty of arming myself with an array of insecticides. Synthetic chemicals can harm the soil and a wide variety of beneficial creatures, some of which are seriously declining in population. We should all be doing our utmost to move over to organic methods of control, including the encouragement of natural predators. Ladybirds, lacewings, frogs, hedgehogs and birds are all adept at limiting numbers of garden pests, such as aphids and slugs. In most but, admittedly, not all instances, there's an organic control worth trying. These include sprays based on plant extracts and various biological controls, which can be introduced on to plants or into compost, ranging from soil nematodes to parasitic wasps that will predate on specific pest species.

Many pests and diseases are prevalent only in certain conditions. During warm, dry weather, for instance, you may barely see a snail, but aphids will multiply at pace. Others only appear at certain times of year. Lily beetles are most devastating in spring and early summer, whereas vine weevil grubs are active throughout winter. Many problems are restricted to certain plants so won't affect everything at once. In time you'll become familiar with what to look out for and when.

Diseases such as rusts, mildews and leaf spots are an inevitable occurrence on certain plants (unless you grow resistant varieties). I either avoid these altogether or limit the number I grow and pick off affected leaves and ditch them if they are badly stricken (but not on the compost heap). Physiological disorders are an occasional problem but are often caused by difficult growing conditions, such as erratic watering, or weather that even gardeners cannot control. And then there are deficiencies, such as chlorosis, that can cause leaf discolouration but are easily remedied once you've worked out the specific shortage.

A favourable aspect of engaging in social media is that you can follow container gardening blogs and posts on information-sharing apps to help problem solve. Gardeners are a sharing community. You can also use camera apps to take close-ups of insects and help identify them.

GOOD HEALTH

Healthy, well-grown and cared-for plants are far more resilient than weak, stressed specimens. They are less prone to diseases and more able to recover from pest attacks. Always check for signs of pest or disease, stress or damage when buying plants. Ensure vine weevil favourites, such as heucheras, are firmly rooted by gently tugging the crown of the plant or tapping it out of the pot. Where possible, choose disease-resistant varieties and avoid or limit the numbers of plants that attract specific pests. For instance, I grow only a few potted lilies as, in my garden, the annual appearance of lily beetles is a certainty. A good air flow, sufficient light and judicious watering will further help resistance. Sap-sucking insects such as aphids are more prevalent on very soft growth.

QUICK GUIDE TO ORGANIC PEST CONTROL

- Draft in beneficial creatures: plant to attract a wide diversity of insects and encourage larger predators by providing them hideouts or habitat (such as log piles for frogs, toads and slow worms).
- Hand picking: pick or wipe off small numbers of pests manually. Snip and bin diseased leaves to reduce the chance of further spread.
- Physical deterrents and barriers: a few common garden pests are sensitive to specific materials (slugs and snails to rough surfaces) and wire mesh buried just below the compost will help protect spring bulbs from foraging squirrels.
- Organic deterrents: many plant oils and other organic-based substances use plants' natural resistance to attack specific garden pests.
- Biological controls: soil nematodes and parasitic wasps will prey on specific pest species; these can be ordered online and delivered to you at the optimum time for use.
- Non-chemical sprays: spray plants with water or a light soft soap solution to dislodge aphids and similar species. Garlic solutions deter slugs and snails.
- Companion planting: certain plants attract predatory pollinators and, often due to their pungent smell, can disguise vulnerable plants to literally throw pests off the scent. For instance, the aromatic leaves of thyme deter blackfly, and marigolds (calendulas) are especially attractive to hoverflies and lacewings.

Slugs and snails are said to be sensitive to copper: self-adhesive copper tape encircling the rim of pots containing slug favourites (such as hostas) is worth a go, especially if combined with other deterrents such as solutions containing garlic applied to the leaves and stems'.

Index

Acknowledgements

I'm indebted to Chloe for the excellent but not easily won additional images in the Planting for Success chapter: photographs it was impossible to take myself!
Thank you.

My great appreciation also to all at Pimpernel Press for their support, especially Anna Sanderson and Gail Lynch for their faith, patience and encouragement throughout and to Jo Christian for picking up and running with the idea. Thanks also to Becky Clarke for making sense of a glut of photographs and putting them artfully on the page and to Penelope Miller for patience and good humour.

Huge thanks also to the many friends, especially Mark, who helped me through to the conclusion of this time-consuming project.

Finally, thank you to the following companies for supplying pots, plants and seeds without which this book could not have happened:

Woodlodge Products Ltd (Suppliers of pots and garden ornaments)
Visit www.woodlodge.co.uk for details of your nearest stockist

The Bransford Webbs Plant Company (Wholesale supplier of quality garden plants)

Mr Fothergill's Seeds Ltd (Seed and young plant suppliers)
Visit www.mr-fothergills.co.uk

Woolmans Plants (Mail order supplier of plants and bulbs)
Visit www.woolmans.com

Adam Christopher Design (Designers and makers of sculptural garden planters)
Visit www.adamchristopherdesign.co.uk